SEVENTEEN MARTYRS

Desmond Forristal

SEVENTEEN MARTYRS

THE COLUMBA PRESS

THE COLUMBA PRESS
93 The Rise, Mount Merrion, Blackrock, Co Dublin, Ireland

First Edition 1990
Design and illustration by Bill Bolger
Origination by The Columba Press
Printed in Ireland by
Genprint Ltd., Dublin

ISBN 1 85607 005 0

ACKNOWLEDGEMENTS

This book is based on documents assembled by the Dublin Diocesan
Commission on Causes for presentation to the Congregation for the
Causes of Saints in Rome. The author is grateful to the Commission
for being given access to these documents, especially to its secretary,
Father Benignus Millet O.F.M., for his assistance and encourage-
ment. Father Fearghal MacRaghnaill O.F.M., and Mr Breandán Mac
Giolla Choille gave valuable help with the illustrations.

CONTENTS

INTRODUCTION

The Christian faith came to Ireland without the shedding of blood. St Patrick's message was received with joy and he himself was honoured and respected throughout his life. In most other countries, the first preachers of Christianity were persecuted and put to death. Their bravery in suffering often had more effect than their words. It was the witness of the Christian martyrs more than any other human cause that brought about the conversion of the Roman Empire. One Roman author summed it up in a memorable phrase: 'The blood of martyrs is the seed of Christians.'

When the Normans invaded Ireland in the twelfth century, they pretended they had come to civilise the barbarian Irish. One arrogant Norman cleric told the Archbishop of Cashel that the faith had never taken proper root in Ireland because of the lack of martyrs. The Archbishop agreed that the Irish had never raised their hands against the saints of God. 'But now,' he said, 'a race of people have come to this land who know well how to make martyrs. From now on Ireland will have martyrs like other countries.'

The Archbishop spoke truly, though it was not until four centuries later that the real age of Irish martyrs began. During the sixteenth and seventeenth centuries the whole of Europe was torn apart by religious conflict. Protestants killed Catholics and Catholics killed Protestants in the name of their respective faiths. In Ireland most of the victims were Catholics, because it was the Protestants who were in power. No one knows the number of Irish men, women and children who died for their religion in that period. It certainly runs into many thousands.

The lives and deaths of seventeen of these martyrs are recounted in this book. Their cause for beatification has recently been introduced in Rome. It is hoped that they will soon be granted the title of Blessed as a first step towards being declared saints. The only thing that sets them apart from so many others is the fact that some details of their sufferings have been handed down to us. They have been chosen to represent a vast army of martyrs. In honouring them, we honour all those others whose sufferings are forgotten and whose names are unknown.

They are a varied group of people. There is one archbishop, three bishops, six priests, a brother, a widow, an alderman, a baker and three sailors. The amount of information we have about them varies. We know a great deal for instance about Archbishop O'Hurley, whose cruel treatment caused horror all over Europe. On the other hand, we know almost nothing about the Wexford sailors apart from their deaths.

In the history of Ireland, religion and politics have always been closely intertwined. There is often difficulty in deciding whether a person was put to death for religious or political reasons. In the case of these seventeen there is no doubt. Some of them were implicated in resistance to the British government and this may have been part of the reason for their arrest. But we know that they were put to death for their religion, either because it was clearly stated or because they were offered freedom and rewards if they would renounce their faith. It was because they stood fast to their beliefs that they died.

There is one danger to be guarded against in reading about these martyrs. Their stories inevitably throw an unfavourable light on those who condemned them. This should not be allowed to give rise to anti-Protestant or anti-British feeling. It was a period when little tolerance was shown by either side. There were Catholic governments in Europe who dealt ruthlessly with those who differed from them in religion. There were Protestant martyrs who chose to suffer and die rather than abandon their beliefs. Cruelty and bravery were to be found on both sides of the religious divide.

The Irish martyrs died without hatred in their hearts. In a number of instances they had the opportunity of publicly forgiving all those who had contributed in any way to their deaths. We honour them for the faith that formed them and the hope that sustained them. Let us honour them above all for the love that they bore for their God, their religion, their country, and their fellow men and women of whatever nationality or religious belief.

Chapter One

THE FIRST MARTYRS

Patrick O'Healy and Conn O'Rourke

SMERWICK HARBOUR is a wide and secluded bay on the tip of the Dingle peninsula, the most westerly point of Ireland. In the sixteenth century it was a favourite landing place for ships from Europe that wanted to avoid attracting the attention of the English authorities. It was a place where smugglers landed their goods, where soldiers brought in arms and ammunition, where priests, who had been ordained in the continental seminaries, returned to their homeland. There was no-one to see them except a few Irish-speaking farmers and fishermen, and they could be trusted to keep a secret.

One day in the summer of 1579 a small boat from Brittany put into the bay. Two men dressed in sailors' clothing left the boat and set off in the direction of Limerick. Their appearance was deceptive.

They were not French sailors but Irish Franciscans. They came from the Co. Leitrim area and had both probably joined the Order of St Francis at Dromahaire Friary, which had managed so far to survive the suppression of the monasteries. They were then sent to Europe for the priestly training that Ireland could no longer provide and now they were returning to minister among their own people. Their names were Patrick O'Healy and Conn O'Rourke.

Patrick O'Healy was the older of the two, having been born about 1545. He studied theology and was ordained priest in Spain, where he soon became known as an outstanding scholar and preacher, as well as a man of great goodness and holiness. In 1575 he visited Rome, seeking help for Sir James Fitzmaurice, an Irish nobleman who was planning what he called a crusade, a military expedition to Ireland in defence of the Catholic faith. Patrick made such an impression on the Vatican officials that he was appointed Bishop of Mayo the following year by Pope Gregory XIII.

His return to Ireland was beset by difficulties. In addition to the normal dangers of travel in those days, there were English spies in the principal cities and ports, watching all who came and went. In the winter of 1577-78 he set sail from Portugal with Fitzmaurice but they were beaten back by storms and had to abandon the expedition. He went on to Paris while Fitzmaurice returned to Spain.

In Paris Bishop O'Healy stayed in the Franciscan Friary and helped in the education of the young friars. Those who met him were struck by his humility and kindness as well as by his intellectual gifts. It was here that he met a young priest name Conn O'Rourke, about five years his junior, a member of the noble family of the O'Rourkes of Breifne. In the spring of 1579 the two set out for Brittany to try and find a ship's captain who would bring them to Ireland. After a long wait, they managed to get a boat. A favourable wind blew them to Ireland and they landed safely in Smerwick Harbour, probably in the month of June.

They chose an unlucky time and place to make their landing. The whole of Munster was in ferment. A mixture of politics and religion had brought the south of Ireland to the brink of rebellion against Queen Elizabeth and her government in Dublin. Elizabeth's policy was to extend her rule to every corner of Ireland and to put an end to the Catholic religion. Every man, woman and child in the country must acknowledge her as their temporal and spiritual ruler, as queen of their country and head of their Church.

The Queen's chief agent in the south of Ireland was Sir William Drury, who had been given the title Lord President of Munster three years earlier. He distinguished himself by his zeal in seeking out those he suspected of disloyalty and putting them to death. In one letter written in 1578 he boasted of four hundred executed in Munster by martial law, that is, without being given a trial or any opportunity of defending themselves. His aim was to terrorise the Irish into submission, but in fact his cruelty was having the opposite effect and driving them into open revolt.

The two men, the bishop and the priest, made their way through the counties of Kerry and Limerick until they came to Askeaton, seat of the Earl of Desmond, the cousin of Sir James Fitzmaurice and the most powerful nobleman in Munster. They hoped that he would give them shelter and help them on their way. Gerald Fitz-Gerald, fourteenth Earl of Desmond, was a descendant of the Norman invaders who came to Ireland in the twelfth century and who in the course of four centuries had become an accepted part of Irish life. They were known as the Old English, to distinguish them on the one hand from the Old Irish, the original inhabitants of the country, and on the other hand from the New English, those who had come to Ireland in Elizabeth's reign and had no understanding or love for the country.

The Earl was known to have little love for Elizabeth's rule or for her religion. He bitterly resented the Queen's attempts to curb his power and as a result of his defiance he had been imprisoned for several years in the Tower of London. He was a vain, melancholy, moody man, irresolute, impetuous and obstinate, a dreamer and a poet as well as a man of action. Yet for all his contradictions he inspired a surprising loyalty among his people, who preferred to be ruled by the FitzGeralds than by the New English land-grabbers.

The ruins of the Earl's house are still to be seen in Askeaton and even in decay they make an impressive sight. The house was both a fortress and a mansion. Built on an island in the river and surrounded by walls and battlements, it was strong enough to withstand a besieging army. Inside the walls was a splendid residence with a vast banqueting hall where the Earl could entertain his guests in kingly style. On this summer's day, the whole place must have been bustling with life and activity. Soldiers, armourers, grooms, artisans, gardeners, victuallers, and a multitude of household servants would all have been busy about their various duties in the the service of the great Earl.

The two travellers asked to see the Earl but were told he was away and were brought to see his wife instead. Eleanor, Countess of Desmond, was an able and strong-minded woman, a kind of Irish Lady Macbeth, far more practical and politically astute than her husband. She could see that the Queen's representatives were trying to force the Earl into a hopeless rebellion so that they could confiscate his vast territories, some of the richest land in Ireland.

The arrival of the two men was an unwelcome shock to her. She feared the effect on the Earl of these visitors from the continent, with their talk of the Catholic counter-reformation and of the crusade to turn back the tide of Protestantism. It was the kind of talk that could turn the Earl's head and involve him in a romantic, doomed rebellion. It was fortunate in her eyes that the Earl was absent and she began to see a way of turning the incident to her advantage.

She gave no inkling of her true feelings to the two newcomers. On the contrary, she welcomed them warmly and pressed them to stay for a while and rest after their travels. They were glad to accept her invitation and they remained there for three days, enjoying the hospitality and comfort of the great house. Then they resumed their journey to Limerick city, where they could take the bridge across the Shannon and continue on through Connacht to the bishop's diocese of Mayo.

They did not know that they were walking into a trap. The Countess had sent a message to the Mayor of Limerick and told him about the two men who were approaching the city. It was meant to prove that she and her husband remained loyal to the Queen. The mayor sent out his soldiers to intercept them and the two were taken prisoner and thrown into Limerick jail.

The old writers are understandably scathing about the action of the Countess in betraying her double trust as a Catholic and as a hostess. 'Beneath her outward show of kindness there did lie treachery, a vice very commonly found in women,' one of them wrote ungallantly. In her defence it could be said that her treachery was no greater than that of the Queen's men who were trying to entrap her. Her first thought was for her husband and her children and for them she was ready to sacrifice two strangers. She could not foresee the fate that lay in store for them, since up to this time no bishop had been put to death for his faith in Ireland.

Bishop O'Healy and Father O'Rourke were only a short time in jail when the threatened invasion took place. It turned out to be something of an anti-climax. Sir James Fitzmaurice landed at Smerwick on the 18 July 1579 with a force of a few hundred soldiers scraped together from various European countries. He established himself at Dún an Óir, a pre-historic fort on a small headland overlooking Smerwick Harbour, and called on the Catholic people of Ireland to rise in rebellion. The English reacted in panic and sent every available soldier to Munster to repel the invasion. Sir William Drury himself made for Limerick and decided to interrogate Bishop O'Healy. He thought that he must have come to prepare the way for the invaders and that he would be able to give valuable information about their strength and their plans.

At his first confrontation with the bishop, Drury decided to try persuasion rather than force. He promised that he would set him free, allow him to take possession of his diocese and heap him with all kinds of honours, on two conditions. One was that he would renounce his faith and become a bishop of the Queen's Church. The other was that he would reveal exactly what his business was in Ireland. The bishop answered firmly that he would not abandon his faith even at the cost of his life, and that his only business in Ireland was to carry out his duty as a bishop by working for the advance of religion and the salvation of souls.

Drury then asked him what plans the Pope and the King of Spain had made for the invasion of Ireland. It is unlikely that the bishop knew much about these plans. He had been a friend and supporter of Fitzmaurice in Rome but he took no part in preparing for the invasion. Even if he did have some information, he was not prepared to say anything that would betray the trust of others or put them in danger. He refused to answer.

Drury decided to use force and ordered him to be tortured. The jailers brought in sharp nails and a hammer and began to hammer the nails into the bishop's fingers. As he still refused to give any more information, the torture was intensified until some of his fingers were torn from his hands. It was all in vain. Nothing that they did could make him speak.

Finally Drury ordered the two men to be put to death. There was no trial, nor could there have been, since they were guilty of no offence except refusing to acknowledge that that the Queen was head of the Church; and that was not a capital offence under Irish law at the time. So Drury simply claimed the right under martial law to dispense with a trial. He declared that the bishop and his companion were guilty of treason and condemned them to be hanged. In reply, the bishop repeated that he and his companion were innocent of any crime and that the sentence was contrary to all law and justice; and he reminded the judge that he himself would have to face the just and all-powerful Judge before long.

Drury left Limerick for Cork and brought the two prisoners with him. They were put sitting on two garrans, small Irish horses, their hands and feet tied, and a strong guard of soldiers surrounding them. If this display was intended to strike terror into the onlookers, it failed in its purpose. The sufferings of the two prisoners and the courage they displayed aroused the sympathy and admiration of all who saw them on their journey. Drury stopped in Kilmallock, a walled town about twenty miles from Limerick which at that time was one of the most important towns in Munster. It was here that he gave the order for the sentence to be carried out.

The prisoners recited the Litany of the Saints and gave one another absolution as they were led to the trees that were to be their place of execution. The bishop added some words of encouragement to the younger man to strengthen him in the face of death. Then he spoke to the crowd which had assembled and urged them to remain steadfast in their faith and in their obedience to the Roman Pontiff. He finished by asking them to pray for him and his companion. The two men were then hanged by the neck until dead. It was about the 13 August 1579.

After their execution, their bodies were left hanging from the trees for a week. During this time they were made the butt of all kinds of mockery and abuse. The soldiers used them as targets to practise their marksmanship, saying, 'Now I'll shoot the Pope's bishop in the head,' or the arm or the leg, and so on. When they had finally tired of their sport, the two bodies were taken down by sympathisers and buried in an unknown grave.

Drury continued on his way to Cork. Soon after this, he was struck down by a sudden and mysterious illness and died on the 3 October. The people saw it is as a just retribution for his crimes and it was rumoured that in his last hours he called upon the martyrs for forgiveness.

Patrick O'Healy was the first bishop to be put to death for his faith in Ireland. Young, vigorous, a man of deep learning and spirituality, he could have made an outstanding contribution to the life of the Church in Ireland at this crucial time. It was not to be. He died without ever setting foot in his diocese. But the way he and his companion died was widely reported and long remembered, and it strengthened many in their commitment to the old religion. In death they achieved what was denied to them in life.

Chapter Two

THE WITNESS OF THE LAITY

Matthew Lambert, Robert Myler, Edward Cheevers, Patrick Cavanagh and companions

The rebellion started by Fitzmaurice gradually spread throughout most of Ireland. Fitzmaurice himself was killed in a minor skirmish soon after landing and the rebels asked his cousin, the Earl of Desmond, to join them and become their leader. Despite the betrayal of the two Franciscans, the English authorities were as determined as ever to bring about the Earl's downfall. On the 2 November 1579 they formally declared him to be a traitor. He had no alternative but to take over command of the rebel forces.

At first the Desmond rebellion met with some success and by the summer of 1580 it had reached Leinster. The leaders there were Viscount Baltinglass, an Old English nobleman, and Fiach Mac Hugh O'Byrne, one of the Old Irish chieftains. O'Byrne's territory lay in the Wicklow Mountains, rugged and roadless, and all attempts by the English to dislodge him ended in failure. Baltinglass was less successful and by the end of the year his forces had melted away and he had to flee for his life. In February 1581, accompanied only by his Jesuit chaplain, Father Robert Rochford, he came to the busy port of Wexford to see if he could find a ship to bring him to the continent.

The wealthy citizens who had been his friends in better days turned their backs on him, now that he was starving and in danger. It was among the poor people of the town that he found refuge. A baker named Matthew Lambert, known as a pious and God-fearing man, received the Viscount and the Jesuit and fed them and sheltered them in his bakery. Meanwhile some seamen, who served on ships that sailed out of Wexford, tried to arrange a safe passage for the two fugitives but met with no success. Baltinglass and Rochford left Wexford and eventually managed to escape from Ireland by another route.

Word of what happened reached the ears of the authorities. The baker and five of the sailors were arrested and thrown into prison to await trial. Matthew Lambert was subjected to long interrogations, threatened with torture and possibly tortured. This simple man, who had never learned to read or write, bore himself with great courage and dignity. To all the questions about matters of politics and religion, to all the arguments about the Pope and the Queen, he gave the same simple answer: 'I am not able to debate with you. All I can tell you is that I am a Catholic and I believe whatever our holy mother the Catholic Church believes.' He was tried, found guilty of treason, and sentenced to be hanged, drawn and quartered.

The familiar phrase 'hanged, drawn and quartered' refers to the most savage method of execution in use at the time. Matthew had to stand in court while the dreadful sentence was spelt out by the judge, in these or similar words:

Matthew Lambert, hear the sentence which the court pronounces upon you: namely, that you, the prisoner at the bar, be conveyed hence to the place from whence you came, and from thence that you be drawn to the place of execution upon a hurdle, that there you be hanged by the neck, that you be cut down while you are still alive, that your privy members be cut off and your bowels taken

out and burnt before your eyes, that your head be severed from
your body, that your body be divided into quarters, and those
quarters be disposed at the Queen's pleasure; and may the God of
infinite mercy have pity on your soul.

On the day appointed, he was placed lying on his back on a kind of
wooden frame called a hurdle and dragged by a horse through the
rough streets of the town to the place of execution. He was taken
from the hurdle, a rope was put around his neck, and he was hanged
from the gallows. While he was still alive and conscious, he was cut
down from the gallows and the mutilation began. A contemporary
description of his death says that while many of the crowd were
weeping he himself showed nothing but joy and continued praising
God until death came to release him from his sufferings.

The same fate awaited the five sailors. The names of only three of
them are known: Robert Meyler, Edward Cheevers and Patrick.Cav-
anagh. They were equally courageous in professing their faith. In
the prison they were subjected to physical torture and emotional
pressure. Their parents and wives were brought into the jail and
allowed to talk to them. This was done not out of kindness but in
the hope that it would weaken their resolve. The attempt was in
vain. At their trial, the men once again publicly proclaimed their
Catholic faith. They were found guilty of treason and condemned
to be hanged, drawn and quartered. All five were put to death on
the same day.

The execution of the baker and the sailors took place in Wexford
in July 1581. The people of the town were in no doubt that their
crime was not treason. It was their loyalty to the religion of their
fathers. From the day of their death, these six working men were
venerated as martyrs for the faith.

Margaret Bermingham

While the baker and the sailors were awaiting trial in Wexford Jail, a brave old lady named Margaret Bermingham was coming to the end of her days in the dungeons of Dublin Castle. The martyrs of Wexford remain shadowy figures to us, with little known about them apart from the circumstances of their death. Not so Margaret Bermingham. The old histories bring her vividly to life and show us a woman of tremendous personality, known to all the people of Dublin for her goodness, her generosity and her unquenchable courage.

Margaret Bermingham was born near Skreen in Co. Meath around the year 1515. As her surname suggests, her ancestry was Old English rather than Irish. In 1530 she married Bartholomew Ball, a merchant in the city of Dublin who was also of Old English stock. It is said that there were twenty children of the marriage, though only five survived into adulthood, three boys and two girls. Her husband's business prospered and his importance in the city grew. He was Mayor of Dublin in the year 1553-54 and died in 1568.

As a wife and as a widow, Margaret was one of the strongest supporters of the old religion in Dublin. She lived through troubled times in the city and saw the Reformation come to Ireland in the 1530s, when the King was declared head of the Church and all the best-loved relics, including St Patrick's crozier, were thrown on to a huge bonfire in Christ Church Place. The years that followed were years of sadness for Margaret as so much that she held dear was swept away and the Mass was banished from the churches of Dublin. Her greatest grief was caused by her eldest son, Walter, who became a convinced Protestant and a determined opponent of the Catholic religion.

Margaret was the head of a large household and she ruled it with skill and prudence. In the manner of the time, the household included many servants and she took a motherly interest in their welfare. Not only did she train them in their duties, she also looked after their spiritual welfare. She made sure that they were instructed in their faith and that they attended prayers every morning and evening.

The servants she trained were in great demand in other houses and when they took up new employment they proved to be apostles as well as servants. Father John Howlin, a Jesuit priest who knew her and visited her house, wrote: 'They were like students graduating from the best of schools. They won over for Christ not only their fellow men-servants and maidservants, but very often their masters and mistresses as well.'

As the persecution of Catholics intensified, Margaret offered a safe house to any bishops or priests who might be passing through Dublin. She was rarely without a priest in the house, which meant that she had the great happiness of attending Mass almost every day. She often invited her son Walter to dinner when there were priests present, in the hope that they would be able to convince him of the error of his ways. It was all in vain. Neither their arguments nor her prayers could win him back.

Margaret's activities were well known but her position and her popularity in the city gave her some protection. Accusations were being constantly made against her, and her house was raided several

times. More than once these raids took place during Mass time and
Margaret and the priest were paraded through the streets on their
way to jail, the priest still dressed in his Mass vestments. By using
her influence and by paying fines or bribes (the distinction between
them was not entirely clear) she always regained her freedom. Each
time the vestments, chalices, missals and so on were confiscated but
she managed to replace them and continue on as before.

The situation changed for the worse in 1580. Two things happened in that year. One was the rebellion by Baltinglass and
O'Byrne in Leinster, which was uncomfortably close to Dublin and
caused great alarm to the English administration. The other was the
election of her son, Walter Ball, as Mayor of Dublin. He decided
that drastic action was needed in order to protect the city from the
dangers of Popery and rebellion. The most obvious and persistent
offender was his own mother. He ordered her to be arrested.

Why did he do it? Needless to say, Catholic writers of the time
denounced him as a monster of depravity, an unnatural son who
turned on his own mother in order to win favour with the government and advance his career. This is a possible explanation, but it is
equally possible he was genuinely convinced that the Catholic religion was false, that the Pope was Anti-Christ and that the Mass was a
blasphemous fable. It was a time when religious passion ran high
and little mercy was shown on either side. To many Protestants he
may have appeared as a man who put his principles above his per-
sonal feelings, according to the teaching of the Gospel, 'He who
loves father or mother more than me is not worthy of me.'

By this time Margaret Bermingham was in her mid-sixties and
crippled by arthritis, though her spirit was as indomitable as ever. As
she could no longer walk any distance, she was put lying on a wooden
hurdle and drawn through the streets by a horse as if on her way to
execution. She was brought to Dublin Castle where she was to be
imprisoned for the rest of her life.

Some of those who were prisoners in the Castle at this period
have left us descriptions of their ordeal. The cells were sited underground, freezing in winter, stiflingly hot in summer. The ventilation
was poor and there was no sanitation, so that the air was perpetually
foul and the stench scarcely bearable. Some prisoners might be

lucky enough to obtain a candle which gave a little light but added to the heat and stuffiness in summer. Otherwise they spent their time in darkness. There was no provision for exercise and no medical care. The prisoner was expected to pay for food or have it sent in from outside.

Margaret Bermingham was an elderly woman. She had spent her life in comfortable circumstances with an army of servants at her beck and call. The conditions of her imprisonment must soon undermine her health and bring about her death. What made it all the harder was the fact that she could leave her prison at any time and return to her comfortable home. All she had to do was renounce her religion and take the Oath of Supremacy, accepting the Queen as head of the Church. It might seem a small thing to do, but to Margaret dying seemed a much smaller thing.

Her friend Father Howlin, who had enjoyed her hospitality so often in happier days, ended his account of her life with these words:

> The unconquerable spirit of this woman, strengthened by faith and hope in Jesus Christ, bore all these things patiently to the end. Worn out by the filth of the prison, by her sufferings and by her infirmities, and leaving behind her the example of a Christian and truly Catholic woman, she fell asleep in the Lord about the year 1584.

Chapter Three

DEATH OF AN ARCHBISHOP

Dermot O'Hurley

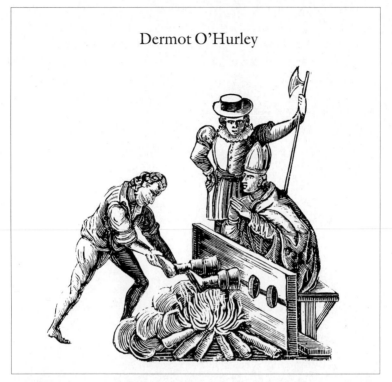

THE BEST KNOWN Irish martyr of the sixteenth century died in Dublin in the same year as Margaret Bermingham. For a time he was her fellow prisoner in Dublin Castle, though there is no evidence that they ever met. He was Dermot O'Hurley, who three years earlier had been appointed Archbishop of Cashel. Like Patrick O'Healy, he died without ever reaching his diocese.

Dermot O'Hurley was born in Emly, Co. Tipperary, about the year 1530. His father was a land-owner and acted as an agent in business matters for the Earl of Desmond, which meant that the family were well-off by the standards of the time. As a young man, Dermot was sent abroad to study at the University of Louvain in Belgium, where he began what was to prove a distinguished academic career. At this time he had no intention of becoming a priest and his interest was mainly in legal studies. He received a doctorate in both civil and canon law and was appointed Dean of the University's law school. After fifteen years in Louvain, he went to the University of Rheims as Professor of Law and spent four years there. Finally, about 1570, he made his way to Rome where he continued to work and lecture in the field of law, and where he soon gained a high reputation, not only as a scholar but as a man of deep faith and outstanding moral character.

In 1581 it was decided to appoint a new archbishop to the vacant see of Cashel. Pope Gregory XIII asked Dermot O'Hurley to accept the position and he agreed. It is hard to say which was the more extraordinary, the offer or the acceptance. A fifty-year-old layman who had spent all his life studying and teaching law seemed a strange choice to be an archbishop. Nor was the position offered an attractive one. Dermot was now in comfortable middle age, a settled and respected member of the academic community. He was being asked to leave this peace and security and return to Ireland, where he would have to live as a fugitive with the ever-present threats of betrayal, imprisonment, torture and death. That the offer was made and accepted says all that needs to be said about the respect in which he was held and the qualities that deserved it.

In the summer of 1581 a series of ordinations brought Dermot through all the grades of the clerical life, the four minor orders followed by the four major orders, subdeacon, deacon, priest and bishop. In September he was formally appointed Archbishop of Cashel and in November he was given the *p   a   l*   - *l   i   u   m*, the sign of an archbishop's rank. It now remained for him to find some safe way of getting back to Ireland and taking up his duties.

It was not until the summer of 1583 that he succeeded in making the journey. In the little port of Le Croisic in Brittany he met a ship's captain from Drogheda who was willing to take the risk of bringing him to Ireland. As a precaution, he sent his baggage and his documents of appointment on another ship, so that if he were captured there would be nothing to betray his identity. His own ship made the voyage safely but the other ship fell into the hands of pirates and the documents found their way to Dublin Castle. By the time he landed in Ireland, the authorities knew he was coming and were already on the watch for him.

Knowing that there would be government spies watching those leaving the ship at Drogheda, he disembarked at Holmpatrick, a little harbour near Skerries. It was his first time to stand on his native soil for more than thirty years. He was met by an Irish priest, John Dillon, who brought him to stay at an inn in Drogheda. At dinner in the inn, he unwisely let himself get involved in a debate about religion with an argumentative Protestant gentleman. He spoke with such force and learning that it was obvious he was no ordinary traveller. A well-wisher told him that he was in danger of betraying his identity and advised him to leave at once. Father Dillon's cousin, the Baron of Slane, had his castle only ten miles away and the two men decided to go there as quickly as they could and ask for shelter.

In the meantime, the Protestant gentleman made his way back to Dublin Castle and reported what he had seen and heard. His name is given as Walter Ball and it seems very likely that he was the same Walter Ball who had so often argued with priests in his mother's house and had recently committed her to prison for her faith. The Castle officials did not take long in putting two and two together and coming to the conclusion that the man in the inn was none other than the newly arrived Archbishop of Cashel. The hunt was on.

Thomas Fleming, Baron of Slane, welcomed the two men and invited them to spend some time in his house. Slane Castle still stands now as it stood then on a hill beside the river Boyne, one of Ireland's largest and stateliest homes. It was easy for the two men to remain out of sight in a private room in the castle while they waited for the hue and cry to die down. After some days, they became bolder and began to appear in public and to eat with the Baron and his guests.

One day a new visitor arrived at the Castle. He was Sir Robert Dillon, a man who graphically illustrates the tangled web of loyalties, political, religious and family, in which so many people of the time found themselves entrapped. Sir Robert was chief justice of the common pleas and a member of the privy council. At the same time, he was a cousin both of the Baron and of Father Dillon. Ambition pushed him towards the new religion, family ties and traditions urged him to hold on to the old. Whose side was he on? His family and friends did not know. He hardly knew himself. It is not surprising that the archbishop, after more than thirty years abroad, found it difficult to know who he could trust.

It is likely enough that Dillon's arrival in Slane was no accident and that he hoped to find out some information about the archbishop. His hopes were soon fulfilled. When the dinner was served, Dermot was among those at table. It was an unwise move, but the Baron probably felt that even if Dillon did recognise him, he could be trusted as a guest and a kinsman not to betray him. In this he was mistaken. The archbishop's name was never mentioned but his bearing and conversation once again gave him away and Dillon was in no doubt who he was. He said nothing at the time but returned to Dublin and reported to the Lord Justices that he had found the man they were looking for. Then he wrote a letter to the Baron telling him to arrest the stranger staying in his house or suffer the consequences.

The Baron was furious at the letter. He had no intention of breaking the laws of hospitality and laying hands upon an honoured and distinguished guest. It was clear to Dermot, however, that it was no longer safe for him to stay in Slane so he decided to make his way south to his diocese of Cashel. He wanted first of all to pay his respects to the Earl of Ormond, in whose territory the diocese of Cashel lay. He had as his travelling companion one of the Earl's illegitimate sons, who had been staying in Slane. They came to Carrick-on-Suir, where the Earl had his principal residence, an old fortified castle to which he had added a new manor-house in the Elizabethan style. It has recently been renovated and today looks much as it did when Dermot O'Hurley visited it in the September of 1583.

Thomas Butler, Earl of Ormond, was generally known as Black Tom, a reference both to his complexion and his character. He was another of those Old English nobles who liked to keep a foot in both camps. He grew up in the royal court in London, where he embraced the Protestant religion. His dark good looks made him a favourite of Queen Elizabeth and some said a lover as well. Back in Ireland, he took the English side against his long-time enemy the

Earl of Desmond in the Munster rebellion and by the autumn of 1583 he had brought the rebels close to defeat. He had shown no mercy to their lives or their property, killing men and burning crops and houses wherever he went. Yet at the same time he had no desire to increase the power of the English Queen in the south of Ireland. He was fighting for himself, not for her. He wanted to live as his forebears had lived, ruling his people in the old way, without dictation from Dublin or London.

Despite his profession of Protestantism, he still retained an affection for the old religion. He greeted the new archbishop respectfully and this respect deepened as he came to know him better. It is said that he asked him to administer the sacrament of confirmation to his young son and heir, James, a sickly child who was feared to be in danger of death. He made arrangements for a house to be put at Dermot's disposal in the town and saw to it that he was provided with food and anything else that he needed.

Dermot was now in a position to see for himself the sorry state of the people of Munster. As a result of the scorched earth policy pursued by Ormond and his English allies, famine and disease were widespread. The English poet, Edmund Spenser, has left us a graphic description of the scenes he witnessed in the wake of the conquering armies:

> Out of every corner of the woods and glens they came creeping forth upon their hands, for their legs could not bear them. They looked anatomies of death, they spake like ghosts crying out of their graves, they did eat of the dead carrions, happy where they could find them, yea, and one another soon after, insomuch as the very carcases they spared not to scrape out of their graves. And if they found a plot of watercresses or shamrocks, there they flocked as to a feast for the time, yet not able long to continue therewithal, that in short space there were none almost left and a most populous and plentiful country suddenly left void of man or beast.

One of the archbishop's first objectives was to restore peace to the region entrusted to his spiritual care. Shortly after his arrival in Carrick, news arrived that the Earl of Desmond had been surprised by some soldiers on the borders of Cork and Kerry. The Earl's chaplain,

Father Maurice MacKenraghty, was taken prisoner and the Earl himself barely escaped. The archbishop began to explore the possibility of making contact with the Earl. He hoped he might be able to negotiate peace terms between him and the Earl of Ormond and so bring the war to an end.

He was equally anxious to reconcile those who were divided by religious differences. He wrote a very courteous letter to that notoriously unprincipled character Miler Magrath, who had been appointed Catholic Bishop of Down and Connor by the Pope and then Protestant Archbishop of Cashel by the Queen. Written in Latin, it is the only one of Dermot's letters that has survived. In it he thanks Magrath for a favour he had done to his sister, Nora, and assures him that he will not try to deprive him of his title of Archbishop of Cashel. He will be content to be known simply as Dr O'Hurley.

> Would that we could meet face to face and speak our minds to one another. Then would it be made manifest how truly I am your friend. Far from desiring to do aught that would harm you or endanger your position, I would be content with my academic title and my family name. I seek to make war on no man. I desire to plant and foster friendship and peace. If you can be persuaded of the truth of this, then will you love me and I in turn will love you and yours. If you invite me to meet you, I will trust in your words, for there are many things we can speak of that may not safely be put in writing.

The letter was dated 20 September 1583. It was never sent because of the sudden arrival in Carrick of a very agitated Baron of Slane. He went first to the house of the Earl, who directed him to the house where Dermot was staying. He had a tale of woe to tell. After Dermot had left Slane, the Baron was summoned to Dublin and accused before the Council of having harboured a notorious traitor in his castle. He was threatened with fines and imprisonment if he did not immediately find the traitor and bring him to Dublin. He begged Dermot to come back with him to the city. Otherwise, he was in danger of being completely ruined.

Dermot agreed to go. It was a scarcely credible decision. Anyone could have told him that he was putting his liberty and his life in

danger. It was true that he had not meddled in politics and was
guilty of no crime in Irish law, but that had not saved Bishop
O'Healy or many others. It is possible he may have seen it as an
opportunity of convincing the Dublin government that he was a
man of peace and that they had nothing to fear from him. It is possible but unlikely. The simplest explanation is probably the true one,
that he did not want the Baron to suffer for his act of hospitality and
that he was willing if necessary to lay down his life for his friend. He
set out for Dublin on the road that led to torture and death, another
Regulus setting out for Carthage. It was the act of either a fool or a
saint, and Dermot was no fool.

Some inkling of what lay in store was given to him when they
stopped in Kilkenny for the night. The Baron was lodged splendidly
in the house of a noble friend. The archbishop was locked up in the
public jail. One of the prison officials was a Catholic and Dermot
spoke to him about the Bishop of Ferns who had recently aban-
doned his faith because of fear. 'Many are lions before the fight,' he
said, 'but in the fight are found to be but stags. I humbly pray the
good Lord that it may not so befall me. For he who thinketh himself
to stand, let him beware lest he fall.'

He arrived in Dublin on the 7 October and was at once imprisoned in the Castle. A few days later the interrogations began. At
that time, the office of Lord Deputy was vacant and the government
was headed by the two Lord Justices, Loftus and Wallop, both Englishmen. Adam Loftus, the Protestant Archbishop of Dublin, was a
weak and ineffectual character, entirely dominated by his more
forceful colleague, Sir Henry Wallop. Wallop had made up his mind
that Dermot O'Hurley was sent by the Pope to encourage and or-
ganise rebellion in Ireland. If he could be made to talk, he would be
able to reveal all the Vatican's plans for overthrowing the Queen's
rule and religion in the country.

The interrogations proved fruitless. Dermot repeated that he
came in peace and that his mission was a purely spiritual one. The
Baron of Slane and Father John Dillon were brought in for questioning but they had nothing to say that would incriminate the prisoner. The Lord Justices began to be seriously worried. They could

not put him on trial, as there was no case against him. They could not release him, as this would be a humiliation for the crown and a triumph for the Papists. They wrote increasingly anxious letters to London asking for instructions about how to proceed.

Instructions soon came from Sir Robert Walsingham, Queen Elizabeth's Secretary of State. He was one of the most sinister figures in that sinister court, a master of espionage and what would now be called disinformation. He specialised in uncovering real or imaginary Catholic conspiracies and was well used to dealing with captured priests in England. His method was to send them to the Tower of London to be tortured on the rack in the hope that they would make some statement incriminating themselves or others. Then they were tried and executed for treason. He told Loftus and Wallop to torture the prisoner until he confessed everything he knew.

This advice was far from welcome to the two Lord Justices. The torturing of an archbishop was liable to cause an outcry not only among the common people, who counted for little, but among the nobles, who were still very much a force to be feared. Even Black Tom, the Earl of Ormond, who had done so much to crush the rebellion in Munster, was known to be favourably disposed towards Dermot. If he were to change sides, the whole country could be lost. The Lord Justices were beginning to be sorry they had ever become involved with the archbishop and their only wish now was to be rid of him. They wrote to Walsingham and offered to send him to be tortured in England:

> But for that we want here either rack or other engine of torture to terrify him and doubt not but that at the time of his apprehension he was well schooled to be silent in all causes of weight, we thought that in a matter of so great importance, and to a person so inward with the Pope and his Cardinals and preferred by them into the dignity of an Archbishop, the Tower of London should be a better school than the Castle of Dublin, where being out of hope of his Irish patrons and favourers, he might be more apt to tell the truth.

Their suggestion met with a cool reception. Walsingham had enough problems in England without importing more from Ireland. He was not prepared to accept their argument that there was no rack or other instrument of torture in Dublin. There were other ways of causing pain that needed no elaborate equipment. He ordered them to 'toast his feet against the fire with hot boots'.

Some time around the end of February 1584 his orders were carried out. A pair of raw-hide boots were brought into the Castle and were thickly coated on the inside with a mixture of salt, butter, oil, tallow and other fats. The archbishop was forced to put his bare feet and legs into the boots and made to sit on a stool with his legs stretched out in front of him, held in position by a wooden stocks. A fire was then lighted under his feet, as described in an early account based on the testimony of eye-witnesses:

> The oil, being brought to boiling by the heat of the flames, caused unbearable anguish to his feet and legs and the like, in such wise that pieces of skin fell from the flesh and pieces of flesh from the bared bones. The officer charged with overseeing the punishment, being unused to such unheard-of torture, did quit the cell of a sudden, lest his eyes look longer on such barbarous cruelty and his ears be affrighted by the cries of the most innocent archbishop resounding through all the neighbouring places.

In his agony, the victim kept crying out, 'Jesus, Son of David, have mercy on me! Jesus, Son of David, have mercy on me!' No other words passed his lips. No confession of guilt, no accusation against his friends, no reproach against his enemies, no renunciation of his faith, nothing except the constantly repeated prayer, 'Jesus, Son of David, have mercy on me!' The torture ceased only when he lost consciousness.

It seemed for a while that he was dead. He was wrapped in a sheet and laid on a feather bed. Some water was forced between his lips and he gradually began to return to life. As the days and weeks passed, he became able to sit up and then to stand and finally to limp a little around his cell.

Apart from bringing the victim to the point of death, the torture had accomplished nothing. The Lord Justices made one last effort to break his resolution. They offered him one of the highest positions in the government service if he would renounce his office of bishop and recognise the Queen as head of Church and State. He refused. They even sent in his sister Nora to talk to him and try to change his mind. He stood firm and bade her to ask God's forgiveness for trying to turn him from the path of duty.

Wallop and Loftus were now very frightened indeed. A note of desperation began to creep into their letters to Walsingham. 'We humbly pray Your Honour to be careful in our behalf,' they pleaded, 'considering in how little safety we live here.' A public trial was more than ever out of the question. It would end with the archbishop's innocence clearly established and their own guilt and cruelty proclaimed to the world. It could be the spark to set off another rebellion. The only solution they could see was to invoke martial law and execute Dermot secretly without trial. Walsingham consulted the Queen and obtained her consent. 'The man being so resolute as to reveal no more matter,' he wrote, 'it is thought meet to have no further tortures used against him, but that you proceed forthwith to his execution.'

On the 19 June, they issued the order for his death. Even under martial law the order was illegal, since martial law could not be invoked against anyone with property worth more than £10. The order was carried out the next day, the 20 June 1584. Very early in the morning, Dermot was taken from his cell and led out of the Castle by the small postern gate. The other prisoners guessed where he was going and raised a great clamour of protest. Among them was a bishop who cried out that he was more deserving of punishment for his sins than the innocent archbishop. Margaret Bermingham may also have been among the protesters if she was still alive. The commotion did not stop until the chief jailer ordered the prisoners to be beaten into silence.

They brought him outside the city walls to Hoggin Green, a stretch of open country near the present St Stephen's Green. It was intended to carry out the execution secretly but just as he was mounting the ladder a group of Dublin merchants arrived unexpectedly upon the scene. They had risen early and come out into the countryside with their bows and arrows in order to have an archery contest. It is to these Dubliners that we owe this description of his last moments found in an old manuscript:

He stood upon the ladder and with great humility and patience uttered these few words following:

"Gentlemen, first I thank my Lord and Saviour Jesus Christ because it hath pleased his divine providence to send you hither to bear testimony of my innocent death, being that it was meant I should die obscurely, as may be seen by sending me to this place of execution so early.

"Be it therefore known unto you, good Christians, that I am a priest anointed and also a bishop, although unworthy of so sacred dignities, and no cause could they find against me that might in the least degree deserve the pains of death, but merely for my function of priesthood, wherein they proceeded against me in all points cruelly contrary to their own laws, which doth privilege any man that is worth ten pound in goods not to die by martial law, which I leave between them and the majesty of the Almighty.

"And I do enjoin you, dear Christian brethren, to manifest the same unto the world and also to bear witness at the day of judgement of my innocent death, which I endure for my function and profession of the holy Catholic faith."   And so desiring them to join with him in prayer, recommending his soul to God his maker and redeemer, most patiently ended his life.

He was put to death by hanging. It does not seem that he was mutilated or disembowelled, but the rope used was made of twisted twigs to prolong and intensify his agony. The Dubliners returned to the city and reported what they had seen and heard to their fellow-citizens. The same old manuscript describes his burial in a way that brings the gospel story to mind:

And when the report of the execution was spread abroad in the city, certain devout women went forth and had his body brought down, which they carried with great reverence unto a little church without the walls called St Kevin's, where he was buried, and his clothes which he did wear was kept among them as relics of his martyrdom.

St Kevin's was an old church, probably built before the coming of the Normans, which had fallen into ruin. After Dermot was buried there, the Catholics of Dublin restored and enlarged the building and made it into a place of pilgrimage. It was said that many miracles were worked and favours granted at his grave and at his place of execution. The remains of the church, which is now once again in ruins, can be seen in a small park in Camden Row, near Kevin Street in Dublin. The martyr's grave is probably within the walls of the church but the exact location is unknown.

Dermot O'Hurley's story is a strange one. A layman enjoying a peaceful and prosperous career in the universities of Europe is suddenly appointed archbishop of a diocese in strife-torn Ireland. A life of steady and unspectacular success ends in a year of tragic and terrible failure. He never even reaches his diocese. After no more than a few weeks of freedom, he is imprisoned, tortured, and put to death. Yet if he had ended his life as a Roman professor, his name would be forgotten. It is because of what seemed like his failure that his name lives on.

His generosity in accepting his appointment, his faith in making his journey home, his selflessness in giving up his freedom to protect his friend, his constancy in professing his religion, his endurance under extremes of physical pain, his grace and courage in the moment of death, these are the qualities that have endeared him to succeeding generations and made his name one of the greatest in the long roll of Irish martyrs.

Chapter Four

THE EARL'S CHAPLAIN

Maurice MacKenraghty

THE DESMOND REBELLION was over by the end of
1583. As a military commander, the Earl of Desmond had
proved to be no match for his adversaries, the Earl of Ormond and his English allies. His only military success, if it can be
called a success, was to attack and plunder the town of Youghal and
then retreat again. From then on one misfortune followed another.
His great castle at Askeaton was besieged and captured, his other
strongholds were taken one by one, his supplies of food and ammunition ran out, his men deserted him in increasing numbers.

In 1580 a contingent of about 600 Spanish and Italian troops
was sent to his assistance by the King of Spain, Philip II. They landed
at Smerwick Harbour in September and entrenched themselves in
Dún an Óir, the old promontory fort which had been used by James
Fitzmaurice the previous year. They expected to be joined by an

Irish army under Desmond's leadership. Instead, they found themselves besieged from land and sea by a superior English force. Out-gunned and out-numbered, they surrendered and handed over all their arms. Thereupon the English commander, Lord Grey, ordered his troops to massacre the defenceless foreigners. Only a dozen or so officers were spared, in the hope that their families would be prepared to pay ransoms for their return.

The Earl of Desmond became a hunted fugitive, protected only by his own wits and the loyalty of his Irish suppporters. He was accompanied by a handful of devoted followers, who refused to abandon him in his misfortune. One of these was Eleanor, his Countess, who shared many hair-breadth escapes with her husband. On one occasion they were surprised at night by their enemies near Kilmallock and the Earl and his wife hid themselves by standing up to their necks in an ice-cold river.

Another faithful companion was his chaplain, Father Maurice McKenraghty. Maurice was a native of the town of Kilmallock, where his father worked as a silversmith. Instead of taking up his father's trade, he chose to study theology in preparation for the priesthood. He obtained the degree of Bachelor of Divinity and was in due course ordained priest.

Kilmallock lay in the territory of the Earl of Desmond. The promising young priest became attached to the Desmond household and was appointed chaplain and confessor to the Earl. When the Earl accepted the leadership of the rebellion in 1579, Maurice accompanied him throughout the campaign and undertook the duties of military chaplain to the fighting men. He remained faithful to his master even when almost all his other followers had forsaken him.

By the summer of 1583 the net was closing around the Earl. In June the Countess parted with her husband and went to the Earl of Ormond in a last desperate attempt to bring about a peaceful settlement. Her attempt was unsuccessful and the hunt for the Earl intensified. On the 17 September some soldiers under the command of Viscount Fermoy came upon a group of about a dozen men in the Sliabh Luachra area, on the border of Counties Cork and Kerry. It was the Earl of Desmond and his last few followers. In the chase that followed, the Earl escaped but his chaplain, who was riding a slower horse, was taken prisoner.

The captured priest was sent to the Earl of Ormond, Black Tom, who ordered him to be confined in Clonmel prison. He sent a letter to London to Lord Burghley, Queen Elizabeth's Treasurer, and informed him of the capture:

> My Lord, if this be the priest that hath been hid with Desmond all this while, he may declare the names of his master's relievers with many other things, and so disclose much treason ... I would this chaplain and I were for one hour with you in your chamber, that you might know the secrets of his heart, which by fair or foul means he must open unto me.

The phrase 'fair or foul means' suggests that the priest was going to be tortured to make him reveal what he knew about Desmond and his supporters. There is no reason to suppose, however, that this was ever seriously intended by Ormond. His real aim in writing the letter was to convince the Queen that he was active in supporting her cause and hunting down her enemies. In all probability, his intention was to keep the priest in Clonmel jail for a year or two until the rebellion was over, and then have him quietly released.

Two months later, on the 11 November, the massive man-hunt came to an end. A group of soldiers, Irishmen in the English service, followed the trail of some stolen cattle to a cave near Tralee. Some men fled as they approached and they entered the cave to find a prematurely aged man, attended by a woman and two boys. It was the Earl of Desmond. One of the soldiers, a man called Daniel Kelly, seized him and cut off his head, the most wanted head in Ireland. The head was sent to Ormond and he in turn sent it to Queen Elizabeth, who ordered it to be displayed on London Bridge. So ended the life and the rebellion of the tragic Earl. He was greatly mourned by the people of Munster, perhaps more than he deserved, for he had brought nothing but misfortune upon them. But they knew that by his death they had lost the last defender of their old religion and their old way of life.

For the whole of 1584 Father MacKenraghty remained in prison in Clonmel. The living conditions were primitive in the extreme, but after his months and years on the run he was well accustomed to hardship. Though he was kept in close confinement, he must have been allowed to receive visitors fairly freely. We are told that he carried out an active apostolate from his prison cell, strengthening the waverers and encouraging the faint-hearted to remain firm in their faith. He urged sinners to turn from evil, to restore ill-gotten goods, to give generously to the poor, to live lives of prayer and holiness. His words were given added force by the example of his own faith and piety and by the patience with which he bore his suffering.

So matters continued until Easter 1585. One of the leading citizens of Clonmel was a man named Victor White, an alderman of the town and a devout Catholic. He approached the head jailer and offered to give him a sum of money if he would release the priest on Holy Saturday night, so that the Catholics of the town could celebrate Easter by going to confession, attending Mass and receiving Holy Communion. The priest would return to the prison on Sunday morning and no-one would be any the wiser. The jailer agreed to the proposal and pocketed the bribe.

As ill-luck would have it, the President of Munster, John Norris, happened to arrive in Clonmel with a troop of soldiers around this time. The jailer, seeing an opportunity of doubling his profits, went to Norris and offered to betray the leading Catholics of the area for a suitable consideration. All that Norris had to do was to raid Victor White's house in the early hours of Easter morning and catch all his birds in one net.

Holy Saturday arrived and Father MacKenraghty was allowed to leave the prison and make his way to White's house, a substantial residence with its own private oratory for the celebration of Mass. As darkness fell, Catholics from all the neighbouring areas began to arrive. Word of the priest's coming had spread and the house was soon filled with people. We have a description of the scene based on eye-witness accounts:

> Now that the long-awaited and joyful hour had come, it was with the greatest zeal that the priest spent the whole of that night in hearing confessions. By early morning all was in readiness for the celebration of Mass. Those of the congregation who had already confessed were divided among the different bedrooms, where they devoted themselves to prayer in preparation for communion.

Others were in the chapel making the altar ready. Others were still being absolved by the priest. The noble Victor was walking in the hall, awaiting the arrival of yet more Catholics, greeting them courteously when they came, bringing them quickly to the chapel, and at once returning to the hall to receive the next comers.

While all this going on, the soldiers were silently making their way through the streets and surrounding the house. Suddenly they burst through the door and found Victor still awaiting his guests in the hall. They arrested him on the spot and then rushed through the house, hoping to catch the priest in the act of saying Mass.

The confusion was indescribable. Some of those in the bedrooms stayed where they were in the hope of being overlooked. Others ran down to the basement to hide themselves. Those who were in the oratory rushed out in disorder, leaving chalice and vestments behind in their panic. Finding the doors guarded by armed men, a number jumped out of windows and some of them were injured in the fall.

Father MacKenraghty himself hid under a heap of straw. The soldiers prodded it with their swords and one of them pierced his leg but he managed to avoid crying out and they passed on. He waited until the hue and cry died down and then succeeded in making his escape. Most of the others were allowed to go, though not until the soldiers had deprived them of their valuables. Victor White was marched off to jail.

What happened next bears a striking resemblance to the capture of Dermot O'Hurley. Victor White, like the Baron of Slane, was threatened with the loss of his property and even of his life unless he could persuade the priest to return and give himself up. But Victor was a braver man than Slane and he steadfastly refused, saying he would rather die than betray the priest.

In his hiding-place, Maurice heard of his friend's danger. He returned to Clonmel of his own free will and surrendered himself to the authorities. He was at once loaded with chains and sent back to his old place of detention, the town jail. This time his fate was in the hands of Norris, not Ormond, and he could expect no mercy.

There is no record of any trial, nor could one have taken place, since the prisoner had not committed any capital offence. Norris simply invoked martial law. He declared him to be guilty of treason and sentenced him to be hanged. He made the offer, usual in these cases, to set the prisoner free and lavishly reward him if he would recognise the Queen as head of the Church. The prisoner rejected the offer and was led to execution.

He was dragged through the streets of Clonmel in the customary way at the tail of a horse. When he came within sight of the place of execution, he asked to be allowed finish the last part of the journey on his knees and this wish was granted. Arriving at the gallows, he spoke to the crowd for as long as he was allowed, urging them to remain always true to their faith and asking for their prayers.

He was hanged for a time from the gallows, cut down while still alive and immediately beheaded. It was the 20 April 1585. For more than a week his head was exhibited over the cross in the centre of the town as a warning to those who might be tempted to follow his example. Then the Catholics, having bribed the appropriate officials, were allowed to collect his remains and bury them in the ruins of the Franciscan church, behind the high altar.

The memory of his death remained alive in Clonmel for many generations. The alley-way off Lough Street where Victor White's house stood became known as Martyr's Lane. The large number of young men from the town who became priests in the years that followed was attributed to the example of Father Maurice McKenraghty.

Chapter Five

A SOLDIER'S TALE

Dominic Collins

AFTER THE DEATH of the Earl of Desmond there was little organised resistance to English rule in the southern part of Ireland. Only the North held out, under the leadership of the O'Neills and the O'Donnells. Young Irishmen from Munster with any ambitions in life had either to conform to English customs and religion or leave their country and seek a career on the continent.

One of those who chose to go abroad was Dominic Collins, a native of the town of Youghal in Co. Cork. He was born about the year 1566 and came from one of the town's leading families. Both his father and his brother served terms as mayor of Youghal. He was given some education as a youth, probably by the Jeşuits, who started a school in Youghal in 1577.

Disaster struck his native town in 1579 when it was captured by the Earl of Desmond and many of its buildings were looted and burnt. The Jesuit school ceased to exist and it was many years before the town regained its former prosperity.

When he was about twenty, Dominic left Youghal to seek his fortune in France. He landed in Brittany with little in the way of money or influence, but with many natural advantages. He was tall, strong, broad-shouldered, good-looking. He had qualities of courage, energy, ambition and leadership. He felt drawn to a military career, for which he was well fitted. But to be an officer he had to be able to arm and clothe himself and own and maintain a good horse. He took a job as serving-man in an inn in the town of Nantes and began to save up his money. Three years and two inns later, he was able to enlist in the army of the Duke of Mercoeur, and he fought on the side of the Catholic League against the Protestant army of the French King Henry IV.

Dominic's military career lasted for nine distinguished years. His moment of greatest glory came when he captured the strategic castle at Lapena in Brittany from the Protestants and was appointed military governor of the area by the Duke. As governor he showed himself to be as honest as he was brave. When the Catholic League began to disintegrate, Henry IV offered him 2,000 ducats to hand over the castle to the Protestants but he refused the bribe. Instead he gave the castle and its surrounding territory to the Spanish general, Don Juan del Águila, who represented the devoutly Catholic King of Spain, Philip II. He then set out for Spain with a letter of recommendation from del Águila and was granted a pension of 25 crowns a month by the King.

He made his way to the important naval base at Corunna in the north of Spain, presumably to continue his military career. But he was becoming disillusioned with the soldier's life and all that went with it. He had always been a deeply religious man and now he began to give himself increasingly to prayer and spiritual reading. It was at this point that he met the man who was to have a decisive influence on his life.

Father Thomas White was a Jesuit priest who had founded a College in Salamanca to educate young Irishmen, especially those studying for the priesthood. He was a native of Clonmel and probably a relative of Father MacKenraghty's friend, Victor White. He has left

us a description of his first meeting with Dominic in the spring of
1598:

> I went to the coast to hear the confessions of Irish soldiers in the
> fleet which was stationed there during Lent. Among them I met
> this officer, Dominic Collins. When I spoke to him he gave
> thanks to Our Lord for meeting a priest who was a member of
> the Society of Jesus and a fellow-countryman. He told me that
> for more than ten months he was unable to feel any joy or inward
> peace by reason of a struggle with Our Lord, who was urging
> him to choose a different walk in life and to leave the world and
> its vanities. He told me he had said this to friars of different
> orders to whom he had made his confession during this time and
> that they had offered to give him the habit of their order and to
> make him a priest or religious, according as he might wish; that
> he had no inclination or desire for what the friars offered him,
> but that when he heard I was a member of the Society he felt an
> inward joy which he could not account for or explain.

Dominic told Father White all about his years of soldiering in
France. During that time he had been in the company of friars who
gambled and swore and behaved like common soldiers. But the Jesuits he met had been different and had impressed him greatly with
their recollection and holiness. It was the dearest wish of his life to
become a member of the Society of Jesus.

Father White was taken by his sincerity and goodness, but he had
to point out the difficulties. Dominic was now in his thirties and had
received little formal education. He could not hope to become a
Jesuit priest, and if he were accepted as a brother he would have to
carry out the kind of duties which would be beneath the dignity of a
high-ranking officer. Dominic was not in the least discouraged. He
would be happy to carry out the humblest work if only he were
accepted by the Society.

Father White agreed to contact the Provincial of the Jesuits on
his behalf. The Provincial thought it unlikely that Dominic could
ever settle down as a brother and was slow to accept him. But
Dominic bombarded him with letters from Corunna until he give in
and agreed to take him on trial. He told him to report to the Jesuit
College in Santiago to begin his period of probation.

Dominic's departure from Corunna was something of a nine days' wonder. The whole military establishment, from the general down, were amazed at his decision to abandon his career and to give up his royal pension. There was equal amazement in Santiago when the tall and handsome Irish officer arrived in full military regalia and proceeded to wash dishes and scrub floors, still wearing his splendid uniform.

His resolution was quickly put to the test. He had barely arrived when the College was struck by plague. Four priests and three brothers were infected and many others fled, fearing that they would catch the disease. Dominic stood his ground and for two months carried out the duties of infirmarian, tending the victims, comforting the last hours of the dying, nursing the others back to health, filling the whole house with the warmth of his cheerful good humour. When the crisis was over, when the dead were buried and the survivors were out of danger and the deserters were making their shame-faced return, there was no longer any question about Dominic's fitness. With the greatest joy he laid aside his soldier's finery and put on the long-desired plain black habit of the Society of Jesus.

Dominic remained two years in the college in Santiago, working in the kitchen, the refectory and the infirmary. A report sent to Rome by his superiors states that he was a man of sound judgement and great physical strength, mature, prudent and sociable, though inclined to be hot-tempered and obstinate – the kind of qualities which might be expected in an Irishman of his age and background. It seemed as if he would finish his days in that peaceful place, having said his last goodbye to the noise of battle and the clash of arms.

Events in Ireland were soon to put an end to this quiet interlude. Once again the country was in turmoil. In Ulster, Hugh O'Neill and Red Hugh O'Donnell were defying the power of the English crown and defeating all armies sent against them. In Munster, James FitzGerald was claiming the title of Earl of Desmond and raising the banner of revolt. The new King of Spain, Philip III, re-solved to send an army to the help of the Irish rebels in 1601. A fleet was prepared and an army assembled in Belem near Lisbon under the command of Don Juan del Águila. Among those travelling with the expedition were the newly-appointed Archbishop of Dublin, Mateo de Oviedo, and the Irish Jesuit priest, James Archer. Dominic Collins was appointed to go with Father Archer as his *socius* or companion. It was a surprising appointment for a newly professed brother and it is possible that he was asked for by del Águila, who was well aware of his abilities.

Once again Dominic found himself surrounded by men in military uniform, though this time he himself was wearing the black habit of a religious. The fleet set sail on the 3 September 1601. The archbishop and Father Archer travelled on the flag-ship. Dominic, who had not yet met Father Archer, followed on one of the supply ships. Like the great Spanish Armada of thirteen years earlier, the expedition ran into bad weather and the ships were scattered. The main part of the fleet landed near Kinsale on the 21 September. Del Águila captured the town and turned it into a fortress for himself and his army of about three thousand men while he waited for help from the northern chieftains.

The section that included Dominic's ship put into Corunna for shelter and when it finally made Ireland on the 1 December it was at Castlehaven, thirty miles west of Kinsale. The local Irish chieftains welcomed the Spaniards. The O'Driscolls handed over to them the castle which gave Castlehaven its name. A contingent arrived from West Cork and Kerry under the command of Donal Cam O'Sullivan Beare, one of the ablest of the Irish leaders. O'Sullivan was on his way to link up with the Spaniards in Kinsale and Dominic joined him, intending to meet Father Archer there. When they arrived they found they could not enter the town as it was now under siege by a large English army under Lord Mountjoy, the Lord Deputy.

The battle of Kinsale is one of the great might-have-beens of Irish history. Comfortably installed in the town was a well equipped Spanish army of three thousand men. Outside it was an English force which outnumbered them four to one but which was suffering from cold, wet and disease in the bleak December weather. Meanwhile, the Irish rebel armies were converging from all directions to join with their Spanish allies. From Tyrone came the great Earl, Hugh O'Neill, from Donegal the dashing Red Hugh O'Donnell, from West Cork the resourceful O'Sullivan Beare. Many others came to swell the Irish forces, which now had the English firmly trapped between themselves and the Spaniards. They prepared for the final onslaught which would put an end forever to English rule in Ireland.

What exactly went wrong with the Irish strategy has never been fully explained. It is said that their plan of attack was leaked to the enemy by a traitor. It is certainly true that they were more used to guerrilla warfare than to the kind of pitched battle which circumstances forced upon them. They made their attack at dawn on Christmas Eve and suffered a humiliating and decisive defeat. Meanwhile, either through indifference or ignorance, Don Juan del Águila and his men remained snugly behind the walls of Kinsale and made no move to help their allies.

The defeated Irish made their way back to their home territories. O'Neill led his army back to Tyrone. Red Hugh O'Donnell gave command of his men to his brother, Rory, and set off for Spain to seek further help. O'Sullivan Beare returned to his lands in Cork and Kerry, where his castle of Dunboy could serve as a centre for further resistance. Don Juan del Águila concluded a gentlemanly peace with Mountjoy, surrendered Kinsale and sailed happily back to Spain with his men. The King of Spain did not share his happiness and had him put under house arrest. He died a short time later.

Dominic Collins accompanied O'Sullivan Beare as he made his retreat. No doubt he recognised O'Sullivan's courage and leadership, qualities which he was to show to the full a year later in his epic mid-winter journey from Kerry to Leitrim. For his part, O'Sullivan must have been glad to avail of Dominic's wisdom and experience, the result of so many years hard campaigning in France. With them went Father Archer, who had escaped from Kinsale. It was the first time that he and Dominic met.

Their destination was the O'Sullivan homeland in the Beare peninsula, a long mountainous spur of land reaching far out into the Atlantic Ocean. Two-thirds of the way along the southern side was a deep safe harbour called Bearehaven, sheltered by Beare Island from the Atlantic rollers. Dunboy Castle, a small square fortress, was sited on a headland overlooking the sea and facing Beare Island. Its guns commanded the strait that led to the harbour and to the little settlement of Castletown. This was the spot that O'Sullivan had chosen to make a last-ditch stand against the English.

O'Sullivan's strategy was to pin down for as long possible the English army, now under the command of Sir George Carew, President of Munster. A picked garrison would hold the castle while O'Sullivan and the remainder of his men would harry the besiegers from the mountains above Castletown. This would give the other Irish chieftains time to regroup and keep resistance alive until the arrival of reinforcements from Spain, which were expected to land shortly. The first part of the strategy worked and the English forces were tied up by Dunboy for six months after their victory at Kinsale. The second part failed, because the Spaniards never came.

The remoteness of Dunboy was part of its strength. To approach it by land, the English would have to fight their way along the mountainous peninsula against guerrillas operating on their native terrain. To approach it by sea, they needed good weather. Instead, they got continuous rain and storms which lasted right up to the end of May. Carew had to write to London to explain the lack of progress and he superstitiously put the blame on Father Archer, who was greatly feared by the English and said to be in league with the Devil.

Archer the priest conjures the foul weather, which I do partly believe, for the old men have never seen the like in May. If he remains in Dunboy, I hope to conjure his head in a halter. He hath a fellow devil to help him, one Dominic Collins, a friar, who in his youth was a scholar and brother to him that was last year mayor of Youghal. Every week he administers the sacrament to them; yet I hope to sow such sedition amongst them that they will break.

Fine weather came at last on the 31 May 1602. Carew marched his men down the Sheep's Head peninsula on the other side of the bay from the Beare peninsula. Then he began ferrying them across to the islands off the coast of Beare. One detachment, which included some Irish loyalists, landed on Dursey Island, overwhelmed the small garrison and butchered all the inhabitants, old men, women and children, to the number of three hundred. The main force landed on Beare Island, which was undefended and directly opposite Dunboy Castle.

On the 6 June they made an unexpected landing on a sandy beach just below the castle. The Irish attempted to resist them but were driven back. Some of them crossed the mountains to join O'Sullivan Beare on the north side of the peninsula, about twenty miles away. Among them was Father Archer. The others, including Dominic Collins, retreated into the castle and the siege began.

The siege of Dunboy Castle was one of the hardest fought in all Irish history. The defenders numbered only 143 men under the command of Richard McGeoghegan. The besieging army numbered at least four thousand and they now had the castle surrounded by land and sea. But it was strongly built and bravely defended. Whenever the besiegers tried to approach they were driven back by gunfire from the battlements and by occasional sallies by the defenders. The English started digging trenches which would enable them to come closer without being hit. The Irish responded by raising earthworks around the castle. Dominic Collins, as a religious, would not have taken an active part in the fighting. But as a veteran of so many battles, he could provide valuable advice and encouragement; as an experienced infirmarian, he could give bodily and spiritual assistance to the wounded and dying; as a Jesuit religious, he could keep before their eyes the cause for which they were fighting, their country and their faith.

The only way the castle could be taken was by artillery, and Carew had come prepared for this. Heavy guns were ferried across and set up in position about a quarter of a mile from the castle. It was slow and laborious work and it was not until the 16th that they were ready to fire. During all this period O'Sullivan Beare, who had at least a thousand men under his command, made no attempt to intervene. He was later accused of callousness and cowardice, though it is possible that he was still hoping for the Spanish troops which would turn the balance in his favour.

At dawn on the 17th the guns began to fire. One of the English officers present wrote an eye-witness account of the bombardment:

On the seventeenth, about five o'clock in the morning, our battery, consisting of one demi-cannon, two whole culverins and one demi-culverin, began to play, which continued without intermission till towards nine in the forenoon, at which time a turret annexed to the castle was beaten down. With the fall of the tower, many of the rebels were buried therein. That being ruined, the ordnance played on the west front of the castle, which by one o'clock in the afternoon was also forced down.

Carew judged that the breach in the castle was wide enough for an assault and ordered his troops to force their way in. A battle of extraordinary ferocity followed, which lasted for the rest of the day. Time and time again, the English rushed the breach and each time were driven back with heavy losses. New waves of fresh troops were brought up but the hard-pressed Irish fought as strongly as ever and showed no sign of wearying. The breach was piled high with bodies and the floor of the castle streamed with blood. Fighting every inch of the way, the defenders were gradually pushed by sheer weight of numbers into the lower part of the castle, a kind of crypt accessible only by a narrow winding stairway. Night was now drawing on and the English did not dare to follow them any further. They contented themselves with placing their flag on the ruins of the castle and withdrew to await what the morning would bring.

It was at this moment, just after sunset, that a tall figure suddenly emerged from the crypt. It was Dominic, who had come out to see if he could arrange an honourable cease-fire on behalf of the defenders. Almost half of the garrison had been killed. Most of the rest were wounded, many seriously. They would be willing to hand over the castle if their lives and safety were guaranteed. The English refused to consider the proposal and Dominic was ordered to be held prisoner.

The following morning the English resumed the attack and started firing on the ruins and into the crypt. As McGeoghegan had been mortally wounded, the Irish chose Thomas Taylor as their new commander. He reluctantly sent out word that the garrison was ready to surrender. When the English entered the crypt to take them prisoner, there was a sudden touch of drama. The dying McGeoghegan rose to his feet, seized a lighted candle and tried to throw it into a barrel of gunpowder. One of the Englishmen seized him and another killed him. The siege was over.

With the example of Dún an Óir still fresh in their memories, the Irish could have had no illusions about their fate. Of the seventy-three prisoners, all that survived of the original garrison, Carew set aside three for questioning, Dominic Collins, Thomas Taylor, and an Irishman of noble birth, Turlough Roe McSweeney. The rest were brought to the market place and hanged, fifty-eight on that day, the 18 June, and the remaining twelve four days later. On the same day Carew gave orders for what was left of the castle to be blown up.

The scant remains of Dunboy Castle stand today on that small headland, facing Beare Island. Grass has grown over the fortifications and cows graze peacefully where so many men fought and died. Three walls of the crypt survive and a part of the stone stairway. In one of the walls is a commemorative tablet with an inscription in Irish. *I gCuimhne na Laoch do thuit i nDún Baoi ar son Tíre is Creidimh Meitheamh 1602 Tógadh an leac so 22adh Meitheamh 1952. Suaimhneas Síorraí d'á n-Anam.* 'In memory of the warriors who fell in Dunboy for fatherland and faith in June 1602 this tablet was erected 22 June 1952. Eternal rest to their souls.'

The three surviving prisoners were brought to Cork to be questioned. Taylor and McSweeney were soon executed, as they had little to reveal. Dominic, a Jesuit lately come from Spain, was thought to be a more promising prospect. Carew interrogated him at length on the 9 July and sent a long report to London on the result of the interrogation. He was forced to admit that it contained little of value. Dominic answered questions about his years in France and Spain and his return to Ireland but nothing he said was of any military importance. There seemed no reason to postpone his execution any longer.

But Carew had other plans for Dominic. Like many English Protestants of the time, he had an almost paranoid fear of the Jesuits. He knew little about them, as is shown by his referring to Dominic as a friar, but he was convinced that they were the chief obstacles to the spread of the Protestant religion. To execute a Jesuit would achieve little. There were plenty of others to take his place. But to persuade a Jesuit to renounce his allegiance to the Pope and embrace the new religion, would be a resounding propaganda victory.

No effort was spared in the attempt to break Dominic's resolution. We are told that he was savagely tortured, though the form of torture is not mentioned. He was promised rich rewards and high ecclesiastical office if he would accept the doctrines of Anglicanism. Ministers of religion were sent into the prison to persuade him of the error of his beliefs. Perhaps the hardest trial of all was when some of his own family visited him and urged him to save his life by pretending a conversion which he could afterwards repudiate. He was in his middle thirties with much to live for. But he turned his back on all these blandishments and chose to suffer a traitor's death.

He was sent to Youghal for execution. It was the first time he had seen his home town in fifteen years. On the 31 October 1602 he was marched through the streets to the place of execution by a troop of soldiers. He wore the black habit of his order, the habit which he had sought so whole-heartedly and loved so greatly. He knelt at the foot of the gallows and greeted it joyfully: 'Hail, holy cross, so long desired by me!' Then he addressed the crowd in a mixture of Spanish, Irish and English, telling them that he had come to Ireland to defend the faith of the Holy Roman Church, which was the one true path to salvation and for which he was about to die.

He was so cheerful that an English officer remarked, 'He is going to his death as eagerly as I would go to a banquet.' Dominic heard him and replied, 'For this cause I would be willing to die not one but a thousand deaths.' His words and demeanour so touched the crowd that the hangman refused to do his work. The soldiers eventually seized on a passer-by, a poor fisherman, and forced him to accept the office. He asked the victim for forgiveness, which Dominic gladly granted before mounting the ladder with the rope around his neck. He was reciting a psalm and had just reached the words, 'Into your hands I commend my spirit,' when the fisherman pulled away the ladder; and so he died.

His body was left hanging for some hours. After a while the rope broke and it fell to the ground, where it was left lying until nightfall. Under cover of darkness, some local Catholics took the body away and buried it in a secret place. From that day on, he was venerated as a martyr in Youghal and his fame gradually spread through Ireland and later throughout Europe. His portrait was exhibited by the Jesuits in Douai and many favours and cures were attributed to his intercession.

It could be suggested in the case of Dominic Collins, and of some of the other martyrs, that the execution was for political rather than religious reasons. But his contemporaries were in no doubt that he was a martyr who had been put to death for his faith. Had he been hanged with the rest of the Dunboy garrison immediately after the siege, there could be some room for doubt. But he was not put to death until more than four months later and it was made clear to him that he could save his life if he renounced his religion. He chose to die and thereby won an honoured place among the Irish martyrs.

Chapter Six

DECISION IN DUBLIN

Conor O'Devany and Patrick O'Loughran

QUEEN ELIZABETH died in 1603. There were great hopes that her successor, King James I, would prove more sympathetic to the Catholic religion: he was, after all, the son of the devoutly Catholic Mary Queen of Scots. The hopes were not fulfilled. Though the persecution of the old religion eased somewhat, the laws remained.

In Ireland, the drive to stamp out all resistance to English rule continued. The government's priority was to establish the King's authority in Ulster, where Hugh O'Neill was still a powerful force. A kind of peace was patched up between O'Neill and the Dublin government in 1603. Two years later the King granted an amnesty to all those who had committed any offences during the years of rebellion. But no-one expected the peace to last.

O'Neill was now growing old and tired and less able to deal with the constant pressure on him from the English government. Settlers brought in from Britain were taking over the rich farmlands of Ulster and driving out the Irish. O'Neill and the other northern chieftains found it increasingly difficult to defend their people against the intruders. They decided to give up the unequal struggle and leave the country.

The exodus took place on the 4 September 1607. On that day the Earl of Tyrone, Hugh O'Neill, and the Earl of Tyrconnell, Rory O'Donnell, together with many of their friends and followers, boarded a ship in Lough Swilly and sailed for the continent of Europe, never to return. It was one of the most traumatic moments in Irish history. *T e i - theadh na n I a r l a*, the Flight of the Earls, was seen by the people as the death-knell of Gaelic Ireland. The last upholders of the old culture and the old way of life had gone. Who would now defend them against the foreigners?

Their fears were quickly justified. Within weeks the government announced that the Earls of Tyrone and Tyrconnell were traitors and that all their lands were forfeit. Plans were drawn up for what was called the Plantation of Ulster, a scheme for replacing all the Irish Catholic landholders by Protestants from Scotland and England. A new drive was made against bishops and priests and many were arrested and jailed. Two of them, Bishop Conor O'Devany and Father Patrick O'Loughran, were to die for their faith.

Conor O'Devany was born about the year 1533. His family were erenaghs in the parish of Raphoe in Co. Donegal, which means that they administered the church property, both buildings and land. As a young man he joined the Franciscans at their friary in Donegal. It is not known where he was ordained to the priesthood: it may have been in Rome. He was certainly in Rome in 1582 when he was appointed Bishop of Down and Connor by Pope Gregory XIII. He was ordained bishop in the Church of Santa Maria dell'Anima on the 13 May and soon afterwards came back to take up duty in his diocese in the north-east of Ulster.

His thirty years as a bishop were to be years of almost continual strife in Ulster. He himself had more than his share of suffering. For much of the time he was on the run, with government spies tracking his movements and plotting his capture. In 1588 he was arrested, escaped briefly and was arrested again. He was brought to Dublin Castle where he spent two years in conditions of great hardship. No charges were brought against him and he was released towards the end of 1590. However, the threat of arrest and imprisonment continued to hang over him for the rest of his life.

During the years of O'Neill's rebellion, the bishop confined himself to his pastoral duties. Unlike some other bishops, he took no part in political affairs. After the Flight of the Earls, he remained in Ireland and by the year 1610 he was the only bishop in the northern part of the country. There was just one other bishop left in Ireland, Archbishop David Kearney of Cashel.

Bishop O'Devany, now in his late seventies, continued to serve his people faithfully and to administer confirmation not only in his own diocese but throughout the country. Secrecy surrounded his whereabouts most of the time but we know that in 1610 he visited Inis na mBeo, the Island of the Living, a famous place of pilgrimage in a lake near Roscrea. It took its name and its fame from an old legend that the bodies of people buried there never decayed. Despite his age, he joined the throngs of pilgrims and made the traditional penitential rounds in his bare feet. The lake is now almost completely dried up and has become the bog of Monahincha, but the little green island with its ancient ruined church still keeps its beauty and atmosphere. It is a place full of memories, not least because it was here that Bishop O'Devany made his last known public appearance before his arrest.

In June 1611 his pursuers finally caught up with him. He was visiting the house of a son-in-law of Hugh O'Neill in order to settle a family dispute. Somehow his presence there became known and the house was surrounded by soldiers. They burst in just after he had finished celebrating Mass, took him prisoner and brought him to Dublin. For the second and last time he found himself a prisoner in the foul dungeons of Dublin Castle.

Father Patrick O'Loughran was arrested that same month. He was a much younger man, having been born about the year 1577. His family were erenaghs in the the parish of Donaghmore in Co.

Tyrone, which was part of Hugh O'Neill's territory. After his ordination to the priesthood, Patrick became one of the chaplains at the great Earl's court. He witnessed the sad decline of his patron in the years following the battle of Kinsale and he was one of those who accompanied him into exile in 1607.

O'Neill spent the last nine years of his life in Rome, where he was honourably received by the Pope and where he died in 1616. Father O'Loughran spent some time with him there, but he was clearly not attracted to an uneventful life in exile when there was so much work to be done by a priest at home. Before going back, he decided to devote some time to study. His education for the priesthood in Ireland had probably left a good deal to be desired because of the disturbed state of the country. He made his way to Flanders and enrolled in the Irish College in Douai, where he filled in the gaps in his theological studies. In the summer of 1611 he returned to Ireland and arrived in Cork in June. He may have been under surveillance by informers, for he was quickly apprehended, questioned and placed under arrest. He was taken to Dublin and imprisoned not in the Castle but in the common jail.

That year of 1611 was a crucial year in the religious history of Dublin. By this time it was clear that the Irish people as a whole had not accepted the Reformation and that the rural population were unshaken in their loyalty to Rome. In Dublin, the issue still hung in the balance. The newly founded Trinity College was committed to Protestantism and was educating young men to be preachers and ministers of the new religion. Their influence was felt especially among the younger generation and it seemed possible that they might turn the tide in Dublin, if not elsewhere. The London government decided to make an all-out effort to end the power of Rome in Ireland, as they had already done in England.

In order to do this, they planned to hold a parliament in Dublin which would pass stronger laws against the Catholic religion. As part of the softening-up process, they instructed the Lord Deputy, Sir Arthur Chichester, to take some dramatic action against the old religion which would frighten the Catholic members of parliament and make it easier to have the laws passed. It was suggested to him that it might be a good idea to put some bishop on trial, as long the trial was for political and not for religious offences. The only bishop in captivity was Bishop O'Devany, so the Deputy ordered him to be charged with treason even though it was known that he had taken no part in any political activities. To make the case look a little more convincing, he decided to have Father O'Loughran tried along with the bishop, since the priest had been chaplain to the so-called traitor, the Earl of Tyrone.

They were the first of the Irish martyrs to be given the luxury of a trial. In treason trials, the balance was weighted heavily against the accused. They were not told beforehand what the charges against them were, they were not allowed to call witnesses or to have a lawyer to defend them. The jury was usually hand-picked to make sure of the verdict. Still, there were formalities that had to be observed. Charges were made, witnesses were called by the prosecution, evidence was presented, the judge made a summing up, the jury were asked to decide whether the defendants were guilty or not guilty. All this took place in an open courtroom, which was generally packed for the occasion. Even if the jury's verdict was a foregone conclusion, the people could hear the evidence for themselves and decide whether justice had been done or not.

The trial of Bishop O'Devany and Father O'Loughran took place in the Court of King's Bench in Dublin on the 28 January 1612. There were two judges, the principal one being Dominic Sarsfield, notorious as a bully and a bigot. He evidently decided that the best way to cover up the weakness of the case against the prisoners was to browbeat them into silence. The bishop was old and frail, the priest was by nature a rather timid man, both were weakened by seven months of harsh confinement. With no lawyers to defend them, they seemed an easy target.

Appearances were deceptive. To the growing delight of the crowd, the two men defended themselves with great skill and courage. The bishop in particular, though he was now about eighty years of age, was so clear in his thoughts and so incisive in his words, that he quickly had the judge on the defensive. He began by objecting to the jury, which contained only one Irishman, the rest being natives of England or Scotland. He pointed out that by law a jury in Ireland must consist of Irishmen. When Sarsfield refused to change the jury, the bishop moved on to a second line of attack. He said that he and his fellow-accused were ordained priests and that no secular court had the right to judge them. He added a quotation from Psalm 105: 'Touch not my anointed ones.'

In an ill-starred moment, Sarsfield attempted to counter one scripture text with another. 'Was not Christ judged and condemned by Pilate?' he asked. The bishop gave a smile of devastating innocence. 'If you are happy to imitate Pilate,' he said, 'then I am happy to imitate Christ.' Then as now, the Dublin crowd loved a quick-witted response. The whole court erupted into laughter and jeers. From there on, the spectators were more than ever on the side of the prisoners.

The rest of the proceedings were a shambles. Now that the judge had cast himself in the role of Pontius Pilate, the trial lost whatever little credibility it had. The charges made against the bishop were ludicrously vague, alleging that he traitorously advised, abetted and comforted Hugh O'Neill, Brian Art O'Neill and other most wicked and criminal traitors in their misdeeds. Since no evidence of this was offered other than the fact that he had at various times met O'Neill and other rebels, the bishop had no trouble in rebutting the charges. Moreover, he pointed out that even if he had plotted with the rebels, he was covered by the amnesty granted by the King in 1605.

The prosecution then produced a witness, a rather pathetic little man, who swore that the bishop had met O'Neill in 1607 and aided him in planning his flight from Ireland. A charge was made against the priest, this time founded on fact, that he had accompanied O'Neill and the other leaders on their flight. Since it was not a crime to leave Ireland, it was difficult to see how such actions could amount to high treason. It was clear, as both the bishop and the priest pointed out, that the trial was not about politics but religion. They were being prosecuted for their faith and for no other reason.

The jury were asked to consider their verdict. They brought in verdicts of guilty against both prisoners. The sole Irish juror disagreed with the verdict, but his protest was set aside even though the law required the verdict to be unanimous. The judge then sentenced the two men to be hanged, drawn and quartered. The execution was set for the 1 February, 1612.

The condemned men were brought to Dublin Castle and confined in separate cells. The Lord Deputy now realised how badly he
had blundered. Instead of striking fear into the Catholic population,
he had given them new spirit and unity. For the four days between
sentence and execution, he sent a stream of emissaries to the prisoners, offering them all kinds of rewards and honours if 'only they
would renounce the Pope and acknowledge the King as head of the
Church.'

The prisoners were unmoved by such blandishments. A woman
who was allowed to bring food to the bishop asked him how he was.
'I have not felt as well in ten years,' he told her. His only fear was
that they might cancel the sentence and leave him to rot in captivity
till his death. He showed her his Franciscan habit, which he was not
allowed to wear, and asked her to do her best to have him buried in
it. 'I put it on as a young man,' he said, 'and I value it more than all
my bishop's regalia.'

The execution took place at about four o'clock in the afternoon.
The gallows was erected on a small hill outside the city on the north
side of the Liffey. At about two o'clock the two men were taken
from the cells, their hands were tied, and they were made to lie face
upwards on two horsedrawn hurdles. 'Christ had to carry his cross
to his execution,' said the bishop cheerfully, 'but I am being carried
to mine.' He had been refused permission to wear his friar's habit,
but he wore it all the same, hidden beneath an outer cloak.

Surrounded by a strong guard of soldiers, they were dragged
through the streets of Dublin and across the bridge to their final destination. Large crowds lined the route and fell in behind the proces-
sion as it passed. Among them were a few Protestant ministers making a last vain effort to convert the condemned men. The vast
majority were Catholics who showed their sympathy openly and
more than once made as if to overpower the soldiers and release the
prisoners. The bishop urged them not to use any violence and blessed
them with his still-bound hands. Many in the crowd knelt to receive
his blessing as he passed, including some of the leading citizens.

Arrived at the gallows, the two were taken from the hurdles and
their hands were untied. The bishop threw off his cloak and stood re-

vealed in his Franciscan habit. They knelt down to pray, their arms outstretched in the form of a cross. Then they approached the gallows and kissed the wooden upright. All the time, the bishop encouraged the young priest to hold firm, afraid that he might weaken.

The public hangman had refused to act and fled the city. His place was taken by an Englishman, a criminal under sentence of death, who was granted his life as a reward. He had sufficient humanity to ask the bishop's forgiveness, which was granted. Then the bishop asked to be executed after the priest, fearing that the younger man might be unnerved by the sight of another's suffering, but his request was refused by the officers. 'You go first,' the priest said to him. ' I will follow you without delay.'

The bishop mounted the ladder and stood on the fourth or fifth rung. He could now be seen by the crowd, estimated at five or six thousand, most of the population of the city. A great cry of grief and sympathy went up from the spectators, followed by a rapt silence as he prepared to address them. He blessed the people again and told them that he had been condemned for his faith and for no other reason. He forgave those who had brought about his condemnation and prayed that God too would forgive them. Then he quoted the words of St Paul: 'If an angel from heaven should preach to you a gospel other than the one we preached to you, let him be anathema.' Fearing how he might develop this theme, the officers hastily ordered the hangman to proceed with the execution. He climbed up the ladder, bound the bishop's hands again and placed the rope around his neck. Those standing nearby noticed that he trembled as he climbed the rungs, whereas the aged bishop had mounted firmly and easily.

At this point something happened which remained imprinted forever on the minds of all who were there. An eyewitness described it in these words:

> It was about four o'clock in the afternoon as the bishop stood there upon the ladder. The sun had not been seen all day, but at that moment it appeared and cast a red light the colour of blood over the whole city and especially over the gallows. It seemed to all those present that such a light could not be natural but must come from some other cause. As soon as the bishop was thrown

down from the ladder and breathed his last, the light disappeared and the sun was not seen again that day.

When the sentence had been carried out in all its barbarity on the bishop, it was the priest's turn. He suffered with equal bravery and composure. He mounted the ladder with the words of Simeon on his lips: 'Now thou dost dismiss thy servant, O Lord, according to thy word in peace.' He blessed the people and forgave all those who wronged him. The rope was put around his neck and he too was thrown from the ladder, cut down, and dismembered.

After each execution, the crowd rushed forward in search of relics, snatching scraps of the victims' clothing and steeping their handkerchiefs in their blood. One man succeeded in stealing the bishop's head after it had been cut off, knowing that the authorities would not allow the remains to be buried in consecrated ground. Despite the offer of a reward of fifty florins, the head was never recovered.

As it was now almost dark, the burial was postponed and a guard of soldiers was left at the scene overnight. On the following day, graves were dug beside the gallows and the remains of the two victims were buried there. All this time, people continued to flock to the place, weeping and praying for the dead men and searching for further relics. When all else failed, they cut pieces from the wood of the gallows and kept them as mementoes. That night, after the soldiers had been withdrawn, a dozen or so young men came from the city, dug up the bodies of the two men and buried them in consecrated ground. The exact location of their last resting place was kept a secret and it remains a secret to this day.

Later historians have described the execution of Bishop Conor O'Devany and Father Patrick O'Loughran as a turning point in the religious history of Dublin. What was intended as a death-blow to the old religion had precisely the opposite effect. The bravery and spirit of the two men, especially of the aged bishop, the manifest injustice of their trial, and the savagery of their execution, could never be forgotten by those who witnessed the events. The tide turned completely against the reformers. Catholics who had been wavering were strengthened and confirmed in their religion. In a letter written to London only five days after the execution, the Lord Deputy himself was forced to admit the complete failure of his scheme. He regretted having to report 'how peevishly and obstinately the cities and corporate towns have of late demeaned themselves, how the priests abound everywhere, who sway and carry this people at their pleasure, how a titular bishop and a priest being lately executed here for treason merely, are notwithstanding by them thought martyrs and adored for saints.'

Francis Taylor

The martyrdom of these two led indirectly to the death of a third martyr in Dublin. The purpose of the Deputy in executing the bishop and the priest had been to frighten the Catholics of the country in the period leading up to the elections for the new Irish parliament. When the elections were held, the first results showed a majority of Catholics who would be opposed to any penal laws. It was only by gerrymandering and vote-rigging that a Protestant majority was eventually secured.

What happened in Dublin was typical. In those days elections were not by secret ballot but by a show of hands. The citizens of Dublin met on the 20 April 1613 to elect their two representatives and they chose two aldermen of the city, Francis Taylor and Thomas Allen. Both men were staunch Catholics. Francis Taylor in particular was known for his loyalty to the old religion and had often offered aid and shelter to priests in his own home.

The Taylors were a wealthy family from Swords in north Co. Dublin. Francis was born about the year 1550. Being a younger son, he did not inherit the land and came to Dublin where he became a leading member of the business community. He married the daughter of another Dublin businessman and had a family of five sons and a daughter. In 1586 he was elected one of the two sheriffs, the beginning of a distinguished career in the service of the city. He was to occupy several other civic offices, including auditor and treasurer, and in 1594 he was elected mayor of Dublin. In 1597 he was one of two envoys sent to London to present petitions to the Queen. He was a man universally respected for his ability, integrity and practical charity.

A man of this calibre could prove very awkward in the new parliament. The mayor, a Protestant, had been absent when Taylor and Allen were elected. He declared the election invalid and ordered a new one to be held. Every obstacle was put in the way of the Catholic party. Some of them were arrested, others were not given notice of the time and date of the election. In spite of this, there was still a majority in favour of Taylor and Allen. The mayor, however, declared that two candidates more acceptable to the government had been elected and these were returned to parliament. Francis Taylor was shortly afterwards arrested and imprisoned.

He spent the rest of his life in captivity. The records do not say whether he was kept in the Castle or in the common jail, but in either place the conditions were extremely harsh, especially for a man of his age and background. No charge was made against him. No trial was held. These things were not necessary. The Lord Deputy had authority to impose sentences other than death by a stroke of his pen on anyone he considered a danger to the state. Francis Taylor was one of these.

It was clear to everyone that the reason for his imprisonment was his religion. Like Margaret Bermingham before him, he could have obtained his release at any time by taking the Oath of Supremacy and acknowledging the King as head of the Church. Like her, he refused. His captivity continued for seven years, the stifling heat of summer alternating with the cold and damp of winter. His health gradually broke under the pressure but his resolution remained as strong as ever.

By the beginning of 1621 he was dying. On the 4 January he made his will, which was witnessed by two of his sons. Even now, the authorities refused to release him. He lingered on to the end of the month and died at 6 p.m. on the 30 January. It was only with great difficulty that his family succeeded in having his body handed over to them for Christian burial. He was probably buried in the Taylor family grave in St Audoen's Church, as he had requested in his will. He was held in honour as a martyr and a lengthy book about his life and sufferings was published in Paris a few years after his death.

The parliament of which he should have been a member proved a grave disappointment to the government. Though the Catholics were in a minority, they resisted the proposed anti-Catholic legislation with great determination and resourcefulness. The parliament was dissolved in 1615 without having passed a single penal law.

Chapter Seven

KING AND PARLIAMENT

Peter Higgins

A NEW KING succeeded to the throne of England in 1625. Charles I was married to a Catholic wife and was much more sympathetic to the old religion than his father had been. For the first 15 years of his reign there was little religious persecution in England or Ireland. But the King's tolerance was resented by the more extreme Protestants and he was accused of having leanings towards Rome.

The period of peace came to an end in the 1640s. A new parliament met in London in November 1640 and it was dominated by opponents of the King. Their opposition was religious as well as political, since they represented the fundamentalist Protestant sects that were grouped under the general title of Dissenters. Their hatred for the Church of England was almost as great as their hatred for the Church of Rome. Within a short while England was divided into two camps, the followers of the King and the followers of the Parliament. Civil war lay just around the corner.

Trouble was brewing in Ireland too. There was particular resentment in Ulster, where Irish Catholics had been driven from their farms and replaced by Protestants from England and Scotland. Rebellion broke out there in October 1641 and spread with remarkable speed to the other provinces. Protestants were driven from the farms they had taken over and fled to Dublin and other towns for refuge. In a number of instances, innocent Protestants were put to death, and there were massacres in which women and children died as well as men.

By the beginning of 1642 the rebels were coming very close to Dublin. They captured the town of Naas and were within twenty miles of the city. Most of the Protestant population took refuge in Dublin but some were unlucky enough to fall into the hands of the rebels. One of them was a clergyman, Canon William Pilsworth, son of the Protestant Bishop of Kildare, who has left us a vivid account of his ordeal.

He was captured by the rebels and brought to the gallows to be hanged. As he stood upon the scaffold, a jeering mob surrounded him and mockingly asked him to preach them a sermon. Just when he had given up hope, a priest suddenly appeared and made a long and impassioned plea to the crowd on his behalf. He spoke warmly of the clergyman's father, the Bishop, who had lived for many years among them and did not deserve that his son should receive such treatment. He warned them that if they put him to death they would draw down God's vengeance upon themselves for their cruelty. The crowd were so moved by his words that they allowed the Canon to come down from the scaffold and make his way to Dublin. He does not name the priest who rescued him, but all the circumstances suggest that he was the Dominican prior of Naas, Father Peter Higgins.

Peter Higgins was born in the Dublin area about the year 1600. His surname suggests that he was one of the Old English who were loyal to the King but remained faithful to the old religion. He joined the Dominican order as a young man and was sent abroad to study. He was probably ordained in Spain about 1625, since he is named as a priest on a list of Irish Dominicans living in Spain in

1627. He returned to Ireland and was appointed prior of the Dominican community in Naas during the period of religious tolerance in the 1630s. He was still there when the rising of 1641 broke out and Naas fell into the hands of the rebels.

During the brief period when the town was under their control, Father Higgins did everything in his power to prevent the kind of atrocities that had happened in other parts of the country. Many Protestants afterwards testified that they owed their lives to his intervention. Sometimes he defended them publicly and used his powers of persuasion to have them set free. At other times, he sheltered them secretly until they could safely make their way to Dublin. A Protestant minister later described how the priest had taken him into his own house and hidden him under his bed until the danger was past. Then he provided him with clothing and money and sent him safely on his way.

Around the beginning of February 1642 two English forces converged on Naas. One was led by James Butler, Marquess of Ormond, the other by Sir Charles Coote, governor of Dublin. Ormond was the commander of the royal army, one of the Old English, a King's man; he had become a Protestant but still maintained good relations with Catholics. Coote was of the Parliament faction, with a fanatical hatred of Catholics in general and priests in particular. Though the civil war between the King and Parliament had not yet broken out, feelings were running very high. Ormond and Coote hated each other at least as much as they hated the rebels.

Ormond was the first to reach Naas. When he entered the town, he found that the enemy had withdrawn. One of the few men left there was Peter Higgins, who was seized by the soldiers and brought to Ormond to be questioned. Finding that the priest had taken no part in the rising and had saved the lives of many Protestants, Ormond promised to protect him.

At this point, Coote and his men arrived. Coote demanded that the priest be handed over to him, which meant certain death. Ormond refused and for a while it seemed as if their followers would come to blows. Eventually, as a kind of compromise, Father Higgins was brought to Dublin and imprisoned there. Ormond informed the two Lord Justices that he was guilty of no crime and that there were plenty of Protestants in the city who would willingly testify to all that he had done for them.

Peter Higgins remained about seven weeks in prison. The conditions he had to endure were harsh, but he had the consolation of receiving three visits from the Dominican prior in Dublin, Father Dominic Nugent, who administered the sacrament of penance to him on each occasion. As there were no charges against him, it seemed likely that he would be released before long. Coote saw himself being deprived of his prey. Out of the blue and all unknown to Ormond, he gave orders for the priest's execution.

Early on the morning of the 23 March 1642 Peter Higgins was brought to the market-place in the city to be hanged. A crowd quickly gathered, and he addressed them, telling them that he was innocent of any crime and affirming his loyalty to the Catholic faith and to the Order of St Dominic. His words were followed by uproar among the crowd, most of whom were refugees from the rebels. Those who knew him shouted that he was innocent and called for his release. Among them was the minister who had hidden under his bed. Those who did not know him howled for his blood, venting on him all their anger against the rebel Irish. Even when the executioner had done his work and the priest had breathed his last, the crowd were not appeased. They stripped his body and subjected it to mockery and abuse. They refused to let it be buried within the city and when it was being carried outside the gate they attacked it and beat it savagely. His final burial-place is unknown.

A relation of Ormond's happened to pass through the market-place and saw what had happened. He immediately informed Ormond, who went to the Lord Justices and demanded that Coote be called to account for what he had done. They refused to take any action and Ormond could do nothing except to denounce Coote's crime and dissociate himself from it. For many Catholics it was not enough. They never forgave Ormond for promising to protect the priest and failing to keep his promise.

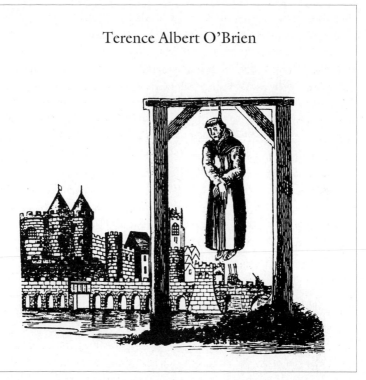

Terence Albert O'Brien

In August 1642 the long-threatened civil war between the King and the Parliament broke out in England. It was reflected in Ireland, where the conflict between royalists and parliamentarians was complicated by two older conflicts, those between Irish and English and between Catholics and Protestants. From 1642 to 1649 most of Ireland was ruled by the Catholic Confederation which had its headquarters in Kilkenny and brought Old Irish and Old English Catholics together under the motto, 'Irishmen united for King, Faith and Country.'

The history of these years is one of constantly shifting factions and alliances, impossible to summarise in a book of this nature. Gradually one force began to dominate the others, the New Model Army of the parliamentary party under its capable and ambitious leader, Oliver Cromwell. The King was defeated and captured and in January 1649 Cromwell signed the warrant for him to be beheaded.

From then until his death, Cromwell ruled England as a dictator. He dispensed with parliament and relied on his army to keep him in power.

Having subdued England, he turned his attention to Ireland. In August 1649 he landed with a strong army near Dublin, which was still controlled by his supporters. He went on to attack and capture the Irish towns one after the other for the remainder of the year. The barbarity with which he conducted his campaign and the hatred which he showed for all who professed the Catholic faith has made his name the most hated one in all Irish history.

He began in September with Drogheda, where his soldiers massacred men, women and children after the town had been taken. A month later he captured Wexford, where similar scenes of slaughter took place. Other towns surrendered or were captured and by the time he returned to England in May 1650 most of the country was under his control. He left his son-in-law, Henry Ireton, to finish the campaign and capture the remaining towns. Of these the most important was Limerick, strongly walled and stoutly garrisoned. Ireton, who had Cromwell's bigotry and cruelty without his military genius, did not begin the siege until June 1651.

One of those in the city at the time was Terence Albert O'Brien, Bishop of Emly. Terence O'Brien was the son of a prosperous landowner and was born in the year 1601 near Cappamore in Co. Limerick. As a young man he joined the Dominican Order at their priory in Limerick city, about twelve miles from his home, and took Albert as his religious name. He was sent to Spain to study theology in Toledo and returned to Ireland in 1627. In that same year he was ordained to the priesthood, though whether this took place in Spain or in Ireland is not known.

He soon earned the esteem of his fellow Dominicans by his character and ability. He served two terms as prior in Limerick and one as prior in Lorrha, Co. Tipperary, an old friary whose remains still survive. In 1643 he was elected Provincial, which made him superior over the entire Irish branch of the Order. The following year he went to Rome to represent Ireland at the General Chapter of the Dominicans. Here he won the respect of the Roman authorities and was soon afterwards appointed Bishop of Emly by Pope Urban

VIII. He spent some time in Portugal, visiting the Irish Dominican houses there, and then returned to Ireland, where he was ordained bishop by the Papal Nuncio, Archbishop Rinuccini.

Emly was a small rural diocese which took in part of the counties of Tipperary and Limerick, including the new bishop's birthplace. It now forms one section of the diocese of Cashel and Emly. In normal times, it would have been a quiet backwater which made no great demands on its bishop; but these were not normal times. War and famine and disease were sweeping through Ireland. Towns were being sacked, churches and monasteries burnt, priests hunted down and killed. Refugees were fleeing from their homes and farmlands before the advance of Cromwell's army. In these times of panic and confusion, the new bishop showed his gifts of leadership far beyond the boundaries of his own diocese. In the words of a contemporary, 'For more than four years he was untiring in his efforts on behalf of his diocese and of the whole Irish church through his authority, his counsel and his vigilance.'

He was in the city of Limerick when the siege began on the 4 June 1651. Ireton was willing to discuss terms with the defenders and he met with their representatives to conduct negotiations. The great obstacle to a cease-fire was his attitude to the Catholic religion. He refused to grant freedom to the Catholics to practise their faith and he continued to threaten death or deportation to any priests who fell into his hands.

As freedom of religion was one of the main demands for which the Catholics had been fighting for the past ten years, the peace talks came to nothing. Terence Albert O'Brien was one of those who were most firm in opposing any surrender to Ireton. His authority both as a man and as a bishop was decisive in persuading the defenders of the city not to yield. Recognising this, Ireton secretly offered him a bribe of £40,000 and a safe-conduct abroad if he would change his position. The bishop refused the offer.

The siege dragged on for almost five months, from the beginning of June to the end of October. Finally it was not force of arms but hunger and disease that decided the outcome. The population of the city was swollen by crowds of refugees and it proved impossible to keep them supplied with food. Then there came an outbreak of bubonic plague, which swept through the narrow streets and carried off many of the starving people. Bishop O'Brien spent much of his time in the plague-house, tending the sick and ministering to the dying. It became clear that the city could not hold out any longer.

The terms of surrender were agreed on the 27 October. Ireton undertook to spare the lives of soldiers and civilians if the city was handed over. He excluded from this offer all Catholic priests and those whose names appeared on a list of twenty men whom he blamed for leading the resistance. One of these was Terence Albert O'Brien.

Ireton's troops entered the city on the 29 October. They had no difficulty in finding the bishop, who was in the plague-house looking after the sick. They seized him, tied his hands with ropes, put iron chains on his legs, and dragged him before Ireton. There was no trial. Ireton roundly abused him for his part in encouraging the city's resistance and ordered him to be hanged the following day.

The bishop spent the night in prison, where he had the opportunity of meeting a fellow-Dominican and making his confession to him. The next day, the 30 October 1651, he was led out to execution. He was followed by a large crowd of citizens, weeping and lamenting the fate of their well-loved pastor. At the place of execution, he mounted the ladder and spoke his last words to his people:

> Keep the faith, follow the commandments, seek nothing but the will of God. By so doing, you shall have eternal life. Weep not for me but rather pray that I be constant and unafraid in this my death-agony and that I bring the course of my life to a blessed finish.

After he was hanged, the soldiers treated his body with unusual savagery. It was left hanging for three hours from the gallows while they beat it with their muskets until it no longer had the semblance of a human form. Then they cut off his head and put it on a spike over the city gate. It is not known when or where his remains were finally laid to rest.

The plague which had helped Ireton to capture the city now proved his undoing. He fell sick shortly after the bishop's execution and his physicians were powerless to help him. In his delirium he cried out that he had not wished the bishop's death but had been forced into it by the military council. 'Would that I had never set eyes upon that Popish bishop,' he kept saying. He died in Limerick on the 26 November.

Chapter Eight

THE HUNTED PRIESTS

John Kearney

THE DEATH OF IRETON did not end the war. Others came to take his place and by the end of 1652 the Cromwellian conquest of Ireland was complete. No-one knows how many hundreds of thousands of Irish died during ten years of constant war, killed in action, murdered in cold blood, carried off by famine and plague. Many others were in exile, fled to the Continent for safety or deported as prisoners to the West Indies.

Those who remained alive in Ireland had not yet come to the end of their sufferings. Cromwell's policy for them was summed up in the famous phrase, 'To hell or to Connacht!' The few Irish Catholics who were still in possession of their ancestral lands were forced to abandon them to English colonists and seek a new home in the infertile country west of the Shannon.

For priests there was still to be no mercy. On the 6 January 1653 a proclamation was issued in Dublin ordering all priests to leave the country under pain of death. Those who gave them shelter were also threatened with severe penalties. A reward of £5 was offered to anyone who gave information leading to the capture of a priest. It was less than the £6 given to anyone who killed a she-wolf but it was still enough to tempt a starving man or woman. Despite the proclamation, many priests refused to leave Ireland and managed to continue their ministry in secret. Inevitably, some were caught and a few paid for their defiance with their lives. Among them were John Kearney and William Tirry.

John Kearney was only thirty-four when he died, but he had packed a great deal of adventure and achievement into his short life. He was born in 1619 in the town of Cashel, where his father was one of the leading citizens. The family were noted for their piety and this influenced the boy from his earliest years. From the age of seven on he attended Mass and said the rosary every day. He was a high-spirited and likeable youth and a great influence for good among the young people of the town.

He grew up in a period of relative freedom for religion. In addition to the parish clergy in Cashel, there was a school run by Jesuits and a Franciscan community living in a private house. By the age of fifteen, John had resolved to become a priest but he found it hard to decide between the Jesuits, from whom he had received his education, and the Franciscans, who were frequent visitors to the family home. Eventually he opted for the Franciscans and, together with his friend and school-mate Joseph Saul, was received into their novitiate in Kilkenny.

After about eighteen months in Kilkenny, it was decided to send the two promising young friars to Belgium for further studies. In Waterford they took a boat for Bristol and on the way ran into an exceptionally violent storm. The story goes that young John led the ship's company in prayers for deliverance, reciting the litany of Our Lady with such fervour that even the Protestant crewmen answered, 'Pray for us.' The storm abated, they reached Bristol, made their way to one of the Channel ports, and arrived safely at their destination, the university city of Louvain.

John Kearney spent the next six years in St Anthony's College, a

Franciscan house of study in Louvain. He followed the usual course in philosophy and theology and was ordained to the priesthood in 1642, at the age of 23. He remained there two more years to complete his studies and then asked permission to return to his homeland. The permission was granted and he set sail once again. This time he took a boat bound directly for Ireland, in order to avoid England which was now largely under the control of the strongly anti-Catholic Parliamentary party.

His second sea journey proved to be even more unfortunate than his first. The ship was captured by Parliamentary pirates and the passengers were brought to Bristol. When it was discovered that John was a priest, he was sent on to London for trial with his hands bound behind his back. In court he admitted and even gloried in the fact that he was a Franciscan priest. On the judge's orders, he was tortured on the rack and had his fingers and toes burnt in an attempt to make him renounce his faith. The attempt failed and he was committed to prison until he should come to a change of heart.

He spent three very harsh months in an underground cell, laden with chains, fed only on bread and water. Here the good-looking young man attracted the attention of the jailer's daughter and she got her mother to ask him if he would marry her. This would have meant breaking his vows as a priest and a religious and would therefore have brought about his immediate release. He refused the offer.

Once again he was brought before the court. In view of his proven obstinacy, the judge condemned him to death. The priest received the sentence with great good humour and even started singing the *Te Deum* until he was forcibly silenced. He was taken to the common jail and put in among the other criminals who were due to be hanged the next day.

The martyr's crown was not yet to be his. A wealthy Catholic gentleman managed to secure his escape during the night, no doubt by handsomely bribing the jailers. He was lowered from one of the prison windows in a basket and brought to his benefactor's house. Here he was provided with food, clothing and money, and in due course he made his way to the coast and succeeded in reaching Calais and safety. A ship from Calais brought him to Wexford, this time without any further misadventure.

Father Kearney's ministry in Ireland was to last for nine years, from 1644 to 1653. In the earlier years, when most of the country was ruled by the Catholic Confederation, he had complete freedom of action. He was appointed to his home town of Cashel, where he taught philosophy and began to acquire a considerable reputation for the eloquence and spirituality of his sermons. His fame as a preacher spread far afield and larger towns started asking for his services. The citizens of Waterford were particularly insistent in their requests and so, after two years in Cashel, he was sent to Waterford to be Master of Novices in the Franciscan friary and principal preacher in their church.

By this time, the political situation was changing for the worse as the Parliamentary party increased in strength. Tragedy struck his home town of Cashel in 1647 when it was attacked by the notorious turncoat Lord Inchiquin, known with good reason as Murrough of the Burnings. Many of the townspeople took refuge in the cathedral on the rock of Cashel and were indiscriminately slaughtered by Inchiquin's men. One of those who died in that day's massacre was Elizabeth Kearney, the priest's mother.

In November 1649 Waterford itself came under attack. Cromwell, fresh from his bloody triumphs at Drogheda and Wexford, arrived at the city and called on the citizens to surrender. They resisted so stoutly that he had to abandon the siege. It was not until the following August that the city surrendered on favourable terms to Ireton. That same month Father Kearney was appointed guardian, or superior, of the Franciscan friary in Carrick-on-Suir.

From now on, as the Cromwellians tightened their grip on the country, his life was the life of a hunted man. His friends urged him to leave the country, at least for a time, but he was not willing to abandon his people in their hour of trial. He continued his work to the best of his ability, constantly on the move, conscious of the danger not only to himself but to all those who sheltered him in their homes. He said Mass wherever the opportunity offered, in houses and cottages and barns, in woodland clearings and on Mass-rocks on the slopes of mountains. A contemporary source describes the last years of his ministry in these words:

Thus it was that Father Kearney remained valiantly in his native land, and by day and by night in the cities, town and villages of Munster did secretly administer the sacraments, console the afflicted, strengthen the wavering in their faith, and to the utmost of his strength sustain those stricken by the plague (of whom there was at that time a great number in Ireland) without any fear or repugnance whatsoever.

The end came early in March, 1653. He was captured in the town of Cashel by an officer called Wilmer and sent under armed guard to Clonmel, which had become the administrative centre of the area. The military governor, Colonel Jerome Sankey, ordered him to be put into the town jail, where there were already a number of Catholic priests and laymen awaiting trial for their religion. These included some Franciscans, who welcomed the newcomer and helped prepare him for the death which now seemed inevitable.

It is evident that the capture of John Kearney was a cause of special satisfaction to the authorities. A leading member of the Order of St Francis, known all over Munster as a teacher and preacher, he was regarded as one of the main obstacles to the spread of Protestantism in the province. No time was lost in bringing him to trial. The day after his arrival in Clonmel, he and the other imprisoned priests were brought before Sankey and charged with treason. Their treason consisted in remaining in Ireland after all priests had been ordered to leave.

The trial centred on Father Kearney. Witnesses were produced who testified that in various parts of Munster he had celebrated Mass, administered the sacraments, and prevented the Catholic people from being converted to the true Protestant religion. As in his trial in London, he made no attempt to deny the charges. He was, he affirmed, a religious of the Franciscan Order and a Catholic priest. It was his duty to celebrate Mass and provide the sacraments for the Catholic people. By doing so, he was committing no crime against the King or against any properly constituted commonwealth. By doing so, he was obeying the law of God, not the iniquitous decrees of Parliament.

Such defiance was not to be tolerated. Sankey brought the proceedings to an abrupt end by pronouncing sentence on the prisoners. Father Kearney was condemned to death by hanging. This was now the penalty for treason, the process of drawing and quartering having been abolished under Cromwell. The other priests (their number is not known) were sentenced to be deported from the country.

The execution took place at eleven in the morning of the following day, Friday, 11 March 1653. For years John Kearney had been forced to disguise himself in the clothing of a layman. Now he put on for the last time his Franciscan habit, with his cord around his waist, his sandals on his feet, his rosary-beads at his side, his crucifix in his hands. As he was led through the streets in this once-familiar garb, he was greeted with tears by some, with mockery by others. At the place of execution, he knelt down and prayed, giving thanks for the death he was about to undergo. Then he climbed the ladder and was given permission to address the crowd. He told them that the only reason for his condemnation was that he had said Mass, administered the sacraments and urged Catholics to persevere in their religion.

> All these things I confessed at my trial; and I not only confess but do affirm that no-one can be saved outside the Catholic and Roman faith, for which faith I gladly die, full of consolation and firmly trusting in the merits of Christ, through which I hope this day to obtain the great reward God has promised to those who love him.

The executioner then pushed him from the ladder and left him hanging until he was dead. His body was not mutilated but was granted to his friends for Christian burial. With great reverence they carried it the fifteen miles to Cashel and laid it to rest in the ruins of the old Franciscan friary. The habit which he had worn was cut up into little pieces for relics, and these found their way all over Ireland and even to the Irish colleges abroad. One of these fragments is still preserved in the Franciscan friary in Killiney, near Dublin.

William Tirry

The hunt for priests continued all during Cromwell's regime. The priest-hunters in the Clonmel area were particularly active and the town jail was rarely without its complement of priests awaiting trial and sentence. Most of them were deported, but the death penalty was still in force and could be applied any time at the whim of the judge. A year after Father Kearney's death another priest was executed in the town. He was the Augustinian friar, William Tirry.

William Tirry was born in the city of Cork in 1608. The Tirrys were an aristocratic Old English family, loyal to the crown and to the old religion. William's father, Robert, occupied a leading place in the civic and commercial life of the city. His uncle William was Catholic Bishop of Cork and Cloyne·from 1622 until his death in 1646. His aunt Joan married Viscount Kilmallock, a staunch royalist and defender of the Catholic cause in Munster.

William was a gifted youth, studious, artistic, a talented writer in both English and Latin. He seems to have been by nature somewhat reserved, strongly drawn to prayer, with a leaning towards the contemplative rather than the active life. After joining the Augustinian Order, he was sent to study abroad, first in Valladolid, then in Paris, finally in Brussels. He returned to Ireland as a priest about the year 1638 and was appointed to the Augustinian community in his native Cork.

His scholarly abilities and his aristocratic connections made it difficult for him to live the life of an ordinary friar in a community. First of all, he was sought by his uncle, Bishop Tirry, who wanted him as his secretary. He accepted the position with some reluctance and after about four months succeeded in resigning and returning to his community. Then his uncle by marriage, Lord Kilmallock, looked for his services as chaplain to himself and tutor to his two sons. Once again he accepted and carried out his duties with his usual care and conscientiousness.

In 1646 he was appointed assistant to the Augustinian Provincial for a three-year term. He seems to have spent the three years in the friary in Fethard, Co. Tipperary, which was then a walled town of some importance. The Augustinian friary and church, built around the year 1300, were still in the possession of the Order. Here he could once again live the community life and join in the community prayers which meant so much to him, especially the daily recitation of the Divine Office in church.

In the summer of 1649 he was appointed prior of the community in Skreen, Co. Meath. That was the summer when Cromwell landed in Ireland and began his conquest of the country by sacking the town of Drogheda, less than twenty miles from Skreen. It would have been impossible for Father Tirry to take up his new appointment and it is likely that he remained in Fethard, where Catholics were still free to practise their faith. That freedom came to an end in the spring of 1650. Cromwell captured the town of Fethard, whose walls were no match for his artillery. The church and friary were destroyed, the friars scattered, the Mass forbidden.

Now began the strangest period of William Tirry's life. In the town of Fethard there lived a relative of his, Mrs Amy Everard, the widow of a wealthy landowner. She invited him to live in her house and act as tutor to her son. He accepted the invitation and spent the last years of his life in her home. As the hunt for priests intensified, it became unsafe for him to leave the house and he remained there as a virtual prisoner. A contemporary source tells us that for three years he lived in one small room, without light, without heat, never setting a foot outside it, seeing no-one unless they came to receive the sacraments. He lived a life of great austerity, rising early in the morning and spending long hours in prayer before celebrating Mass. Prayer continued during the day, mingled with reading and writing. He studied the writings of Protestant theologians and began writing a book which would refute their teachings and set out the essentials of the Catholic faith.

It sounds a bleak existence yet he does not seem to have been unhappy. He was a scholar who loved the company of his books and his confinement gave him a rare opportunity for serious study. As he had always lived a mortified life, the lack of comfort did not much concern him. The absence of light and heat was something he accepted as penance for his sins, though it probably originated as a safety precaution. A light in his window or smoke coming from his chimney could draw attention to his presence in the house.

The life he led there is in marked contrast to the lives of other priests in the area, men like John Kearney who kept moving one step ahead of their pursuers, saying Mass and administering the sacraments in houses or in the open air, according as the opportunity offered. Was Tirry guilty of cowardice in choosing such a hidden existence for himself? Or did he judge that he was by birth and temperament unfitted for life on the run and that he would be recognised and captured as soon as he left his hiding-place? It is certain that he bore himself with great bravery in the end when he came face to face with death. And even during his years in hiding he showed no lack of courage. He remained in Ireland when he could have found safety abroad, and he continued to minister to those who came to see him though he knew the risks involved.

As the years passed, more and more people in the area came to know of the priest in Mrs Everard's house and quite a few had visited him. But it was not until early in 1654 that word reached the ears of the authorities. Three of the locals, tempted by the miserable reward on offer, turned informer. On the morning of Holy Saturday, 25 March, he had just vested for Mass when a group of soldiers with drawn swords burst into the room and took him prisoner. They bundled him out of the house and brought him to the prison in Clonmel, surrounded by a strong armed escort. With them they took the manuscript of the book he had been writing, which they found upon his desk.

There were already four diocesan priests in the prison awaiting trial. One of them, Canon Walter Conway, described with some amazement how Father Tirry's arrival raised their spirits and altered their lives:

> As soon as he entered the prison, he changed it by a happy trans-formation into a place of prayer. There with the other four he would recite the Divine Office at the accustomed hours, omitting none of the bows or other ceremonies however small that are used in recitation by a large community. He had a pyx containing the Blessed Eucharist and no day passed in all the five weeks he spent in prison that he did not receive viaticum from Father Walter Conway, canon of the metropolitan church of Cashel, having first made a general confession with plentiful out-pouring of tears.

Stories about the new prisoner began to spread in Clonmel and farther afield, eventually reaching the ears of another hunted priest, Father Matthew Fogarty, a Capuchin friar. On the 18 April he himself was captured and imprisoned with the others. He too has left us an eyewitness account of Father Tirry's prayer, not only the devotions which he shared with the other priests but also the long hours of private prayer which he began in the early hours of each day:

> First therefore every morning between 3 and 4 of the clock he would get up roundly and put on his apparel with all expedition, and soon after fall to his prayers on his knees and there continue till 8 o'clock, still either praying, weeping or striking his breast through sensible contrition, to the great edification of all his fel-low prisoners, to the admiration and conversion to a better life of all the hearers, both ecclesiastical and laymen, yea, sectaries and papists, not only in the town of Clonmel but also further in the

towns and villages throughout all of Ireland, as far as the bruit and rumour of his holy life were spread.

On the 23 April the four diocesan priests were tried and sentenced to be deported from Ireland. Three days later the two religious priests, Fathers Tirry and Fogarty, were brought to St John's Church to be tried. This was a formal trial, with a judge, a prosecutor and a jury. Father Tirry was asked why he had not left Ireland when the proclamation was issued. He answered that he had come to Ireland in obedience to his religious superior and could not leave without his permission. 'What?' said the prosecutor, 'Do you acknowledge any higher power in this kingdom than our power?'

'In temporal matters,' the priest replied,' I acknowledge no higher power in this kingdom of Ireland than yours. But in spiritual affairs wherein my soul is concerned, I acknowledge the Pope of Rome and my own superiors to have greater power over me than you others.'

The judge then asked the specially picked jury to consider their verdict. In a great display of impartiality, he told them to take the bible in their hands and swear that they would come to a just and equitable decision. The display was rather spoilt when the foreman of the jury was heard whispering to him, 'Shall we find them all guilty?' 'Who doubts it?' the judge answered, 'What else is to be done?' The jury obediently trooped out and trooped back again with a verdict of guilty on the two priests. Thereupon the judge pronounced the sentence: 'You shall be led from hence to the place whence you came, and from thence to the gallows, when the order shall be given, and be hanged by the neck till you expire.'

They were taken back to the prison, but that night the chief jailer, Richard Rouse, who was evidently a good-hearted man, brought them to more comfortable lodgings in his own house while they were awaiting execution. The people of the town were allowed to visit them and they came in large numbers to receive the sacraments from the future martyrs and to ask their prayers. Many of them left alms, which Father Tirry promptly gave away. He arranged to have forty-six loaves of bread distributed to the poor in atonement for the sins he had committed during the forty-six years of his life. He himself barely ate enough to keep himself alive.

The constant stream of visitors meant that he had scarcely a moment to himself. It was only by cutting short his hours of sleep that he was able to find some time for prayer. 'Sleep is the thief of time,' he used to say. The usual offers of freedom and wealth were made to him by the authorities, if he would agree to change his religion. They can hardly have been surprised when he rejected their offers.

On the 1 May the jailer brought word that he was to be executed the following morning in company with a Catholic layman named Peter Power. Father Fogarty's execution was deferred and was later changed to deportation. The reason why Father Tirry alone of the priests was put to death seems to have been that he was captured when about to celebrate Mass, which was regarded with particular hatred by the Dissenters, and that he had been writing a book to combat their teachings. The reason for Peter Power's sentence is not known.

Father Tirry spent his last night on earth in almost continuous prayer. He would only agree to lie down for an hour's rest on the bare floor in order to have the strength to deliver his last sermon to the people. At about nine in the morning of the 2 May 1654 the soldiers came for him, put iron manacles on his hands and led him to the door of the house. He was refused permission to have Canon Conway accompany him so he received his last absolution from him in the doorway. Then he stepped into the street, wearing his black Augustinian habit, his hair newly tonsured, his rosary beads in his hands.

His walk through the streets of Clonmel became a triumphal progress. He seemed more like a king coming to take possession of his kingdom than a criminal going to his death. Crowds lined the whole route, plucking at his robe, lamenting his misfortune, kneeling for his blessing. He continually made the sign of the cross over them with his manacled hands. When he reached the place of execution there were at least a thousand gathered there to hear his last words.

Peter Power was the first to die, having received absolution from the priest. Then he himself mounted the ladder with the rope around his neck and began a long and eloquent discourse. He spoke about the Catholic Church and the salvation it offered through the commandments and the sacraments. He urged all those present to remain true to the faith which had been brought by St Patrick fourteen hundred years ago. The crowd listened in rapt attention and many of them were in tears. A minister from one of the dissenting sects could bear it no longer and demanded that he be hanged at once before he led any more people astray. Rouse, who was acting as executioner, ignored the man and told Father Tirry he could continue as long as he wished.

The minister then tried to start an argument with him and challenged him to prove that Christ was really present in the Eucharist. Somewhat wearily, the priest referred him to Matthew 26 and First Corinthians 11 and went on, 'I pray you give over to trouble me now at the hour of my death. Go to my comrades whom I left at home and they will resolve you, if you have any more difficulties.'

Having come to the end of his discourse, he pronounced his forgiveness for the three who had betrayed him and prayed for them with all his heart. He asked any priest who might be in the crowd to grant him absolution. Then he gave a sign to the executioner, who pulled away the ladder and left him hanging.

As soon as he was dead, the crowd surged forward in search of relics, tearing pieces from his habit and dipping their handkerchiefs in the blood that gushed from his nose. It seemed for a while as if they would actually dismember his body in their excitement. It was with some difficulty that the mayor of Fethard, a Catholic, succeeded in rescuing it from their enthusiasm. He arranged to have it brought with appropriate solemnity to Fethard, where it was buried in the ruins of the friary. For many years the local people continued to visit his grave and pray for his intercession as a saint and as a martyr. In the nineteenth century the friary church was rebuilt by the Augustinians and it is still in use, but the exact location of Father Tirry's grave is no longer known.

EPILOGUE

CROMWELL DIED IN 1658. Two years later the monarchy was restored and Charles II, son of the executed king, returned in triumph to London. He was even more sympathetic to the Catholic religion than his father and was received into the Catholic Church on his deathbed. He was powerless, however, to control the strange outbreak of persecution that erupted in England in 1678 as a result of the imaginary Popish Plot. Among the many victims were two more Irish martyrs. Blessed Charles Meehan, a Franciscan priest, was executed in Wales in 1679. St Oliver Plunkett, Archbishop of Armagh, was put to death at Tyburn in London in 1681. He was the last person to die for the Catholic faith in Britain or Ireland, the last of the martyrs.

It was not the end of the persecution of the Catholic Church in Ireland. All during the eighteenth century, the infamous penal laws laid heavy burdens upon the Irish Catholics. They were deprived of civil rights. They were excluded from Parliament and the professions. They were denied education in their own religion. They were forbidden to build public churches. They were subjected to economic discrimination. In brief, they were snared in a net of legislation designed to keep them in poverty and in ignorance.

But there were no more martyrs. The English government had found from bitter experience that making martyrs did not work. The death of a martyr did not terrify others into giving up their faith. Rather it strengthened their commitment and encouraged them to greater loyalty. The words of the old Roman were seen to be true. The blood of martyrs is the seed of Christians.

The story of the seventeen martyrs shows why and how this happened. It is good to recall the lives and deaths of those who went before us and made us what we are. Their stories still have the power to touch and inspire us today.